Celebration Series

Lessons from Old Testament Prophets

Editorial Staff

Richard M. Davis . . . . .Editor
P. D. Buford . . . . .Associate Editor

Editor in Chief
United Pentecostal Church International

Robin Johnston

Writers

Larry Arrowood

Robert Bentley

Lorin Bradbury

Brent Brosam

Donald Eddins

Doug Ellingsworth

Robert Gilstrap

B. E. Hart

Dan Long

Timothy Mitchell

David Norris

Garry Truman

Timothy Whistine

Curriculum Committee

James E. Boatman

Donald Bryan

P. D. Buford

Daniel L. Butler

Steve L. Cannon

Richard M. Davis

Jack C. Garrison

G. W. Hassebrock

Robin Johnston

David L. Reynolds

Charles A. Rutter

Rick L. Wyser

The gift of the Holy Spirit is like no other gift God has given to man. This gift is the capstone of the new birth. Further, it empowers individuals to be witnesses (Acts 1:8) and is an integral part of the kingdom of God.

—Lesson 2, page 17

Adult Teacher's Manual

Summer 2013

Table of Contents

WORD AFLAME PUBLICATIONS
United Pentecostal Church International

www.wordaflame.org

Adult Teacher's Manual
Editor: Richard M. Davis • Cover Design: Dennis Fiorini • Design: Karen Myers
Manufactured in USA, June 2013, 194311.

Lessons from Old Testament Prophets

by Richard M. Davis

Our study this quarter is titled *Lessons from Old Testament Prophets*. We could have called it a study of the Minor Prophets, since the lessons come from the prophecies of those prophets most scholars call the Minor Prophets. However, many of us resist that label. Minor in whose eyes? Certainly, they were not minor in the eyes of God who called them to deliver tough messages in tough times!

Of course, whoever coined the designation "Minor Prophets" meant no disrespect, I am certain. The term has been used for many years by educators and scholars alike who were only trying to distinguish between several prophets whose writings were lengthy and a number of prophets—twelve, to be exact—whose writings were limited and short.

That the writings of these twelve prophets were comparatively short, however, in no way diminishes their import. Further, their prophecies were vital both to the people of the kingdoms of Judah and Israel and also to those of us who occupy these days of the church of Jesus Christ. Some of their prophecies are yet to be fulfilled in the end times—the times in which we appear as a church to be approaching quickly.

Perhaps we have failed to teach from these prophecies as often as we should have. There are many wonderful lessons we may glean from these smaller, but potent books of Scripture.

From Hosea we will learn of God's unconditional love for us through a picture of how Hosea dealt with his unfaithful wife. We will study prayer through the prophet Joel. We also will learn lessons concerning the judgment of God, the Lord's desire to restore and revive those who fall away from His will and purpose, and the essential nature of obeying God. Nahum will remind us of God's hatred of sin. Habakkuk will remind of how important it is to place our unwavering trust in God, and Zephaniah will help us to remember how vital hope is to every believer. As Paul said, without hope we are "most miserable."

From Haggai we will realize we do not have to continue living under the curse of sin and disobedience. Rather, we may exchange the curse of sin for the blessing of God in our lives!

Zechariah helps us to remember the accuracy of biblical prophecy regarding Christ's birth in Bethlehem—His first coming—and gives us faith to trust the prophecies that point to His return and millennial reign on earth.

Finally, Malachi reminds us once again how important it is that we honor God in all things, and also that we honor our neighbors, loving them "as ourselves."

We may sometimes refer to these prophets as the Minor Prophets, but there is definitely nothing minor about the roles they played in the lives of God's people then or in the lessons they leave for us today!

Hosea— Unconditional Love

1
week of
06.02.13

Lesson Text

Hosea 1

1 The word of the LORD that came unto Hosea, the son of Beeri, in the days of Uzziah, Jotham, Ahaz, and Hezekiah, kings of Judah, and in the days of Jeroboam the son of Joash, king of Israel.

2 The beginning of the word of the LORD by Hosea. And the LORD said to Hosea, Go, take unto thee a wife of whoredoms and children of whoredoms: for the land hath committed great whoredom, departing from the LORD.

3 So he went and took Gomer the daughter of Diblaim; which conceived, and bare him a son.

4 And the LORD said unto him, Call his name Jezreel; for yet a little while, and I will avenge the blood of Jezreel upon the house of Jehu, and will cause to cease the kingdom of the house of Israel.

5 And it shall come to pass at that day, that I will break the bow of Israel in the valley of Jezreel.

6 And she conceived again, and bare a daughter. And God said unto him, Call her name Lo-ruhamah: for I will no more have mercy upon the house of Israel; but I will utterly take them away.

7 But I will have mercy upon the house of Judah, and will save them by the LORD their God, and will not save them by bow, nor by sword, nor by battle, by horses, nor by horsemen.

8 Now when she had weaned Lo-ruhamah, she conceived, and bare a son.

9 Then said God, Call his name Lo-ammi: for ye are not my people, and I will not be your God.

10 Yet the number of the children of Israel shall be as the sand of the sea, which cannot be measured nor numbered; and it shall come to pass, that in the place where it was said unto them, Ye are not my people, there it shall be said unto them, Ye are the sons of the living God.

11 Then shall the children of Judah and the children of Israel be gathered together, and appoint themselves one head, and they shall come up out of the land: for great shall be the day of Jezreel.

Focus Thought

The steadfast love of God never runs out in spite of our sin.

Focus Verse

Hosea 3:2

So I bought her to me for fifteen pieces of silver, and for an homer of barley, and an half homer of barley.

The Supreme Virtue

by Gary D. Erickson

Sacrificial love is the supreme virtue of the human heart. It is the glue that holds societies together. It is the bond that holds husbands and wives, parents and children, and friends and associates. It is from the deep roots of love that the stalk of harmonious human relations springs. Humanity has the capacity to exhibit many redeemable acts of goodness, but Paul declared love to be the most magnificent virtue of all: "And now abide faith, hope, love, these three; but the greatest of these is love" (I Corinthians 13:13, NKJV). Making sacrifices for others without expecting anything in return is the noblest of all human actions.

Where does this superlative virtue come from? It is not a product of humanness, but a vestige of God's image in us. It is a residue of God's goodness that remained in humankind after the Fall. That's why even atheists can love their children and perform acts of kindness. They were created in the image of God (Genesis 1:26-27). Even though they are not saved or members of God's kingdom, still they are created in God's image. The born-again believer's capacity to love has been increased by the empowerment of the Holy Spirit. Jesus said, "By this shall all men know that ye are my disciples, if ye have love one to another" (John 13:35). Love is the ultimate test of the Christian faith: "He that loveth not knoweth not God; for God is love. In this was manifested the love of God toward us, because that God sent his only begotten Son into the world, that we might live through him" (I John 4:8-9).

I. A PICTURE OF ISRAEL'S UNFAITHFULNESS
   A. Jezreel
   B. Lo-ruhamah
   C. Lo-ammi
II. REJECTION AND RESTORATION OF ISRAEL
   A. The Ugliness of Sin
   B. Love Is Strong as Death
   C. A New Covenant Relationship
III. THE REDEMPTION OF HOSEA'S WIFE
   A. A Demonstration of Love
   B. A Demonstration of Redemption

Contemplating the Topic

The third verse of "The Love of God," penned in 1917 by songwriter Frederick M. Lehman, beautifully depicts the love of God for His people.

Could we with ink the ocean fill,
And were the skies of parchment made,
Were every stalk on earth a quill,
And every man a scribe by trade,
To write the love of God above
Would drain the ocean dry.
Nor could the scroll contain the whole,
Though stretched from sky to sky.

The first three chapters of the Book of Hosea relate a love story of faithfulness demonstrated in the face of betrayal and then renewal. The story allegorically portrays God's unconditional love for Israel, but beyond that, it speaks of God's unconditional love for all humankind.

In response to the Word of the Lord and at great emotional and monetary expense to himself, Hosea participated in a divinely scripted drama that depicted God's unconditional love. God told this godly, faithful man to "take yourself a wife of harlotry and children of harlotry, for the land has committed great harlotry by departing from the LORD" (Hosea 1:2, NKJV). Hosea loved his wife, Gomer, and her unfaithfulness created within him an intense emotional storm of disgust and longing.

We cannot read the Book of Hosea without detecting the tension that existed within the heart of God; His abhorrence for Israel's adulterous ways clashed with the passionate, husbandly love He felt for the nation. God said, "And I saw, when for all the causes whereby backsliding Israel committed adultery I had put her away, and given her a bill of divorce; yet her treacherous sister Judah feared not, but went and played the harlot also" (Jeremiah 3:8). But after a time His everlasting love overpowered His indignation.

"For thy Maker is thine husband . . .
thy Redeemer the Holy One of Israel

. . . . For a small moment have I for-saken thee; but with great mercies will I gather thee. In a little wrath I hid my face from thee for a moment; but with everlasting kindness will I have mercy on thee" (Isaiah 54:5-8).

It is encouraging to note that though God may be angry and disgusted by the sins of His people, His love never diminishes. When a person turns to the Lord in repentance, is baptized in water in Jesus' name, and receives the Holy Spirit, it is as though he never had sinned.

"If the wicked will turn from all his sins that he hath committed, and keep all my statutes, and do that which is lawful and right. . . . All his trans-gressions that he hath committed, they shall not be mentioned unto him: in his righteousness that he hath done he shall live" (Ezekiel 18:21-22).

Searching the Scriptures

I. A PICTURE OF ISRAEL'S UNFAITHFULNESS

At the Lord's prompting, Hosea searched for a wife among the harlots. "So he went and took Gomer the daughter of Diblaim" (Hosea 1:3). Their first child appears to have been fa-thered by Hosea because the Scripture states Gomer "conceived, and bare him a son" (Hosea 1:3). However, it is probable the two younger children were fathered by other men, as the Lord called Gomer "a wife of whore-doms" (Hosea 1:2) and declared, "I will not have mercy upon her children; for they be the children of whoredoms" (Hosea 2:4).

Gomer must have trifled with Hosea's af-fection by flirting with other men, conceiving their children, and returning to Hosea to give birth. Gomer was not aware of it, but she was playing the role of unfaithful Israel, Hosea was depicting the unconditional love of the Lord, and the names of the children exemplified God's impending judgment upon Israel: *Jezreel*, "I will avenge"; *Lo-ruhamah*, "I will no more have mercy upon the house of Israel"; and *Lo-ammi*, "Ye are not my people, and I will not be your God."

Transparency / 1

Transparency 1 quotes a portion of Hosea 1:10.

A. Jezreel

"Call his name Jezreel; for yet a lit-tle while, and I will avenge the blood of Jezreel upon the house of Jehu, and will cause to cease the kingdom of the house of Israel. And it shall come to pass at that day, that I will break the bow of Israel in the valley of Jezreel" (Hosea 1:4-5).

Hosea 1:4-5 encapsulates a great deal of history. Jehu had been used of God to execute a horrendous massacre upon the house of Ahab. (See II Kings 10.) Though Jehu acted in accordance with God's will in destroying the wicked house of Ahab, he in turn became equally wicked in his worship. Immediately after Jehu's initial obedience, God promised him four generations of his children would sit on the throne of Israel, and He kept that prom-ise. Sadly, Jehu's pleasure in the promise did not lead to faithfulness to God. (See II Kings 10:30-31.) "Jehu . . . departed not from the sins of Jeroboam, which made Israel to sin" (II Kings 10:31). Thus, the name Jezreel fore-told vengeance on the dynasty of Jehu.

Israel had strayed far from serving God in truth. Isaiah, whose ministry to the southern kingdom of Judah concurred with Hosea's ministry in the northern kingdom, described the backslidden state of Israel. "The priest and the prophet . . . are out of the way through strong drink; they err in vision, they stumble in judgment" (Isaiah 28:7). God had no pa-tience with religion; He was looking for holi-ness in His people. "And ye shall be holy unto me: for I the LORD am holy" (Leviticus 20:26).

B. Lo-ruhamah

As commanded by the Lord, Hosea named the second child born to Gomer, a daughter, Lo-ruhamah. The name literally means "She that never knew a father." She was an "orphan not by death, but by her mother's sin" (George Adam Smith in *The Expositor's Bible: The Minor Prophets*). By naming the daughter Lo-ruhamah, God declared to Israel the depth to which the nation had stooped in degradation, or as John Calvin described, "Ye are then the offspring of debauchery" (*A Commentary on The Twelve Minor Prophets*).

In retrospect, one cannot help but see the demonstration of the love of God toward His people. He had given more than sufficient warning. Again and again He forgave their re-peated backsliding until He reached the end of His mercy (Hosea 1:6). As God's longsuffering had produced no change in Israel's behavior, there was nothing left but judgment.

However, judgment also can deliver the grace of God. In the case of the Corinthians, the behavior of at least one church member had degraded to the point Paul saw no option but to "deliver [the man] unto Satan for the destruction of the flesh, that the spirit may be saved" (I Corinthians 5:5). The purpose of Paul's action was not vengeance, but unconditional love.

C. Lo-ammi

Finally, a third child, a son, was born to Gomer. God declared this child should be christened Lo-ammi. According to George Adam Smith, the name meant "not my people" or "no kin of mine." Just as Hosea recognized the child was not his, God no longer recognized Israel as His own. There can be no worse position for a nation or an individual than for God to turn His back on them.

Samson provided an explicit example of the consequences of flirting with sin until God turned His back. "And [Samson] awoke out of his sleep, and said, I will go out as at other times before, and shake myself. And he wist not that the LORD was departed from him. But the Philistines took him, and put out his eyes, and brought him down to Gaza, and bound him with fetters of brass; and he did grind in the prison house" (Judges 16:20-21).

Unfortunately, many Christians have repeated this scenario. They dabble in sin and then return to an altar and pray for renewal in the Holy Ghost. Feeling relieved that God forgave them, they return to their pet sins. Since their prayers are more regret than remorse, there comes a day when God closes the windows of Heaven and places a sign on their hearts: "You are not my people, and I am no longer your God." Though God's love is unconditional, there comes a judgment day. Jesus warned of that day in His parable of the ten virgins, five of whom were barred from entering the marriage feast because the oil in their lamps had run out. They pleaded with Him to open the door, "but he answered and said, Verily I say unto you, I know you not" (Matthew 25:12). In other words, "You are not my people; you are no kin of mine."

II. REJECTION AND RESTORATION OF ISRAEL

Chapter 2 of Hosea centers on reflections concerning the problems presented in chapter 1 and God's plans for restoration.

A. The Ugliness of Sin

"The implications of sin are serious, not trivial. Some may feel that their good deeds, church membership, or baptism assures them of a positive relationship to God. They presume that their sins and lack of exclusive devotion to God will not interrupt his love for them. Hosea's theology raises questions with anyone who has a cavalier regard for sin. Sin is a destructive power and a deadly force that interrupts a person's relationship with God. In the eyes of God, sin is like prostitution" (Gary V. Smith in *The NIV Application Commentary: Hosea/Amos/Micah*).

A broken relationship between husband and wife is never pretty. Any child who has experienced the aftermath of his parents' divorce knows the ugliness of that broken relationship. God used the trauma in the lives of Hosea and Gomer to make it clear to the people of Israel that the unfaithfulness rested not on their Father, but upon the shoulders of their "mother." "Plead with your mother, plead: for she is not my wife, neither am I her husband: let her therefore put away her whoredoms out of her sight, and her adulteries from between her breasts" (Hosea 2:2). The Lord used Hosea's tragic marriage to show Israel He had remained faithful to the marriage covenant, even though they had not.

In Hosea's prophecy, God called the children to plead with their mother concerning her adulterous ways. Though the Word of God is clear concerning respect for authority, each child of God bears the responsibility to plead the cause of righteousness. The problem is not new and the plea for righteousness is not old fashioned. Jude admonished, "Earnestly contend for the faith which was once delivered unto the saints" (Jude 3). Peter wrote, "Be diligent that ye may be found of him in peace, without spot, and blameless" (II Peter 3:14).

The secret lies in the willingness of individuals to deny ungodliness and worldly passions, and to live self-controlled, upright lives in this present age while we wait for "that blessed hope, and the glorious appearing of the great God and our Saviour Jesus Christ; who gave himself for us, that he might redeem us from all iniquity, and purify unto himself a peculiar people, zealous of good works" (Titus 2:13-14).

B. Love Is Strong as Death

Solomon wrote, "Love is strong as death" (Song of Solomon 8:6). Though we sense the pain of betrayal in the second chapter of Hosea, one cannot help but plainly see the level of intimacy the Lord maintained for his wife, Israel. Her unfaithfulness, her debauchery, her filthiness could not reduce God's love for her. Instead of rejecting her and erasing all hope of her redemption, He pursued her until, as a prodigal wife, she recognized the benefit of a loving covenant relationship.

"Therefore, behold, I will hedge up thy way with thorns, and make a wall, that she shall not find her paths" (Hosea 2:6).

Hosea 2:6 depicts how God symbolically would "hedge in" His wife like a rancher would hedge in a farm animal next to a stone wall or corral made of thorn bushes. By loving and just discipline, He would bring pressure to bear upon her waywardness until she decided, "I will go and return to my first husband; for then was it better with me than now" (Hosea 2:7).

Transparency 2

Transparency 2 depicts Gomer and quotes a portion of Hosea 2:7.

Hosea's pursuit of his beloved wife would cause her to recognize the Lord and not Baal as God. (See Hosea 2:8.)

Divine discipline is instructive and bears the redemptive purpose of changing the way people think and act. Using the language of romance, the Lord determined to woo His wife back. He put pressure on her through affliction, then led her to a place where He could speak tenderly to her and she would listen.

"Therefore, behold, I will allure her; and bring her into the wilderness, and speak comfortably unto her" (Hosea 2:14).

Many individuals have come to the Lord only when the things of this world were stripped away through trial and tribulation. Only then were they able to hear the tender voice of the Lord calling them home.

C. A New Covenant Relationship

Some people conform to a Christian lifestyle as though it is merely a set of manmade rules. They outwardly comply with God's expectations only out of grudging obedience. They seem to wish God had never found them. But Hosea voiced God's promise that when Israel returned, the nation would relate to the Lord and the world around them in an entirely different way. "At that day, saith the LORD, . . . thou shalt call me Ishi [husband]; and shalt call me no more Baali [master]" (Hosea 2:16). The one who lives for God out of fear will likely stray back to the old lifestyle. Love is the only thing strong enough to keep a believer faithful until death.

Hosea also prophesied the establishment of a new covenant between the Lord and Israel. "I will betroth thee unto me for ever; yea, I will betroth thee unto me in righteousness, and in judgment, and in lovingkindness, and in mercies" (Hosea 2:19). Today the New Covenant promises a total transformation of sinful humankind. "Therefore if any man be in Christ, he is a new creature: old things are passed away; behold, all things are become new" (II Corinthians 5:17).

Love is the only thing strong enough to keep a believer faithful until death.

The third promise prophesied by Hosea consisted of a promise of blessings while in this world. (See Hosea 2:21-23.) As Israel's husband, the Lord promised to meet all of her needs. The church in the New Testament under the New Covenant is granted great and precious promises. As a result of this relationship, we have become "heirs of God, and joint-heirs with Christ" (Romans 8:17). If we need provision, healing, comfort, or reassurance, we can take it to our "husband"—Jesus Christ—who has promised to meet all our needs. "But my God shall supply all your need according to his riches in glory by Christ Jesus" (Philippians 4:19).

III. THE REDEMPTION OF HOSEA'S WIFE

Hosea 3 demonstrates God's unconditional love for the backslider; and in a broader sense, it speaks of God's plan for redemption of all mankind. God is not willing that any should perish, and this chapter illustrates the length to which God will go to save the sinner.

A. A Demonstration of Love

"Then said the LORD unto me, Go yet, love a woman beloved of her friend, yet an adulteress, according to the love of the LORD toward the children of Israel, who look to other gods, and love flagons of wine" (Hosea 3:1).

There is little doubt the unnamed woman in Hosea 3:1 is Gomer, Hosea's wife. *The Amplified Bible* renders Hosea 3:1, "Go again, love [the same] woman [Gomer] who is beloved of a paramour and is an adulteress, even as the Lord loves the children of Israel, though they turn to other gods and love cakes of raisins [used in the sacrificial feasts in idol worship]."

Love is not feeling; love is commitment.

The Lord instructed Hosea to go and love his wayward wife "according to the love of the LORD toward the children of Israel" (Hosea 3:1). Whether or not Hosea felt love, he demonstrated love. There is an important distinction between feeling love and demonstrating love. Husbands and wives who truly love one another demonstrate love to one another whether they feel it or not. Exhausted parents demonstrate love to their children when they are beyond feeling. It is almost certain Jesus did not feel like going to the cross, but love drove Him there and kept Him there until the price for mankind's sins was paid.

This lesson needs to be taught again and again to a generation that believes they are entitled to be loved according to a worldly definition of love, a generation that is able to get out of a marriage almost easier than they got into it. Love is not feeling; love is commitment. As a reminder, it is good to return to I Corinthians 13.

"Charity suffereth long, and is kind; charity envieth not; charity vaunteth not itself, is not puffed up, doth not behave itself unseemly, seeketh not her own, is not easily provoked, thinketh no evil; rejoiceth not in iniquity, but rejoiceth in the truth; beareth all things, believeth all things, hopeth all things, endureth all things" (I Corinthians 13:4-7).

Whether we are loving a spouse or reaching out to a backslider, God calls us to demonstrate love.

B. A Demonstration of Redemption

Transparency / 3

Transparency 3 quotes Hosea 3:2.

The word *redemption* means "to buy back." Hosea said, "So I bought her to me for fifteen pieces of silver, and for an homer of barley, and an half homer of barley" (Hosea 3:2). We do not know how many times Gomer was unfaithful to Hosea, but it is almost certain two of his three children were conceived through illicit relationships with other men. Hosea went to the streets to redeem his wife, a practicing prostitute.

It is true Hosea's demonstration of love and redemption of Gomer served as an object lesson for the nation of Israel. However, its message and lesson extend far beyond the nation of Israel. Imbedded in that chapter is a Messianic promise: "Afterward shall the children of Israel return, and seek the LORD their God, and David their king; and shall fear the LORD and his goodness in the latter days" (Hosea 3:5).

God, who directed Hosea to go to the street where he originally found his wife and buy her back, was the same God who donned a robe of human flesh and entered the world of sinful man to redeem His bride. However, the price He paid to redeem His wife from the clutches of sin was far greater than the silver Hosea paid for Gomer.

"Forasmuch as ye know that ye were not redeemed with corruptible things, as silver and gold, from your

vain conversation received by tradition from your fathers; but with the precious blood of Christ, as of a lamb without blemish and without spot" (I Peter 1:18-19).

Thank God for more than a demonstration of redemption. Thank God for redemption. "For when we were yet without strength, in due time Christ died for the ungodly" (Romans 5:6). "Blessed be the Lord God of Israel; for he hath visited and redeemed his people" (Luke 1:68).

Internalizing the Message

Gary V. Smith asks, "Do people today believe their unfaithfulness in their love affair with God is as serious as a charge of prostitution?" (*The NIV Application Commentary: Hosea/Amos/Micah*).

Jesus told a parable of a son who requested his inheritance and journeyed far from home. Living a riotous life among prostitutes and revelers, he squandered his portion of the resources his father had worked a lifetime to build. When the money was spent and he was destitute, he decided to return to his father's house and offer to be a servant.

The father demonstrated love both by preparation for his return (a robe, a ring, a fatted calf) and by running eagerly toward his son when he spotted him in the distance. "But when he was yet a great way off, his father saw him, and had compassion, and ran, and fell on his neck, and kissed him" (Luke 15:20). The father in the story did not ask for his money back, and he did not put his son on probation. Instead, he held a feast in honor of his son's return. "For this my son was dead, and is alive again; he was lost, and is found. And they began to be merry" (Luke 15:24).

The Book of Hosea is the story of a prodigal wife. In this story, instead of the father waiting patiently for his son to return, the husband searched for the wife of his youth. It is a demonstration of grace—unmerited favor. The scenario served as a message of God's unconditional love for backslidden Israel.

However, the message was not to Israel only; it is for all humankind. Like Gomer, who had apparently sold herself into prostitution and could not free herself from that bondage, we all were locked in the bondage of sin. "For when we were yet without strength, in due time Christ died for the ungodly" (Romans 5:6). Our husband—Jesus Christ—came into this world to seek the lost, and He paid the price necessary to deliver us from the bondage of sin. He demonstrated unconditional love in that He did not come to condemn us, but to deliver us from our sins and give us everlasting life. (See John 3:16-17.)

REFLECTIONS
- Discuss ways in which God's unconditional love impacts the life of a Christian.
- We see in the story of Hosea that God considers unfaithfulness to Him as serious as the charge of prostitution. Discuss.
- Holiness of heart and life is more important to God than religious exercise. Discuss.
- Discuss how trials, tribulations, and judgment can deliver the grace of God.
- Discuss the difference between the feeling of love and the demonstration of love.
- Hosea was a type of Christ. Discuss.

2
week of
06.09.13

Joel—Prayer

Lesson Text

Joel 2:12-17

12 Therefore also now, saith the LORD, turn ye even to me with all your heart, and with fasting, and with weeping, and with mourning:

13 And rend your heart, and not your garments, and turn unto the LORD your God: for he is gracious and merciful, slow to anger, and of great kindness, and repenteth him of the evil.

14 Who knoweth if he will return and repent, and leave a blessing behind him; even a meat offering and a drink offering unto the LORD your God?

15 Blow the trumpet in Zion, sanctify a fast, call a solemn assembly:

16 Gather the people, sanctify the congregation, assemble the elders, gather the children, and those that suck the breasts: let the bridegroom go forth of his chamber, and the bride out of her closet.

17 Let the priests, the ministers of the LORD, weep between the porch and the altar, and let them say, Spare thy people, O LORD, and give not thine heritage to reproach, that the heathen should rule over them: wherefore should they say among the people, Where is their God?

Focus Thought

The universal formula for revival is fasting and earnest, passionate prayer.

Focus Verse

Joel 2:32

And it shall come to pass, that whosoever shall call on the name of the LORD shall be delivered: for in mount Zion and in Jerusalem shall be deliverance, as the LORD hath said, and in the remnant whom the LORD shall call.

Beseeching God with Intensity

by Gary D. Erickson

One of the most biblical and sincere acts of showing contrition and devotion to God is fasting and prayer. Self-abasement is practiced by many religions in a variety of strange ways: self-flagellation, cutting the flesh, abstinence from satisfying normal drives, wearing specific garments, performing rituals, endearing relics, and reciting arcane mantras. For the Christian, fasting and prayer is the biblical precedent for beseeching God with intensity. Self-abuse is not a biblical practice. Neither is placing confidence for spiritual power in objects, ceremonies, or religious recitations. Our bodies are temples of the Holy Spirit and should not be defiled by harmful actions. Even fasting should be done with discretion (i.e., by not abandoning health concerns).

We are all driven by natural desires. Fasting is a way the human volition can take control of our lives. Instead of following our sensual cravings to satisfy hunger, fasting takes control of our flesh. In this way we restrain our human fallen nature and allow the Holy Spirit more influence (Romans 6:6). Paul explained spiritual subjection in the following way: "I am crucified with Christ: nevertheless I live; yet not I, but Christ liveth in me: and the life which I now live in the flesh I live by the faith of the Son of God, who loved me, and gave himself for me" (Galatians 2:20). Sacrifice coupled with prayer can be a powerful tool for seeking God.

"Two passions beat within my chest; the one is foul, the other blessed. The one I love, the other I hate; the one I feed will dominate" (Anonymous).

I. DESCRIPTION OF THE LOCUST PLAGUE
II. DESCRIPTION OF THE ENEMY INVASION
III. DIVINE APPEAL TO JUDAH TO REPENT
  A. The Lord Calls on People to Repent
  B. Repentance Must Be More Than
     Outward Ritual
IV. DECLARATION OF A FAST
V. DIVINE DELIVERANCE PROMISED
  A. Material Prosperity
  B. Destruction of the Enemy
  C. Pouring Out of God's Spirit
  D. Signs Preceding Christ's Second Coming
  E. Judgment of Gentile Nations
  F. Restoration and Future Blessing of the Jews
VI. THE DESCRIPTION OF JOEL'S REVIVAL
  A. A Sweeping Revival
  B. A Weeping Revival
  C. A Reaping Revival

Contemplating the Topic

For some Pentecostals, the prophet Joel is primarily known for the portion of his prophecy Peter quoted as he preached on the Day of Pentecost: "And it shall come to pass in the last days, saith God, I will pour out of my Spirit upon all flesh." (See Acts 2:16-21.) That portion of Joel's prophecy is indeed significant, but the three chapters Joel wrote contain a much broader contribution to God's church.

Joel supplied a glimpse into God's pattern for world-impacting revival. This revival not only touches God, but it moves Him to provide miraculously for His children.

The essential element in God's pattern for revival is passionate and sincere prayer. Complacent individuals often overlook this message, but those yearning for a powerful move of God will find direction through the anointed writings of the prophet Joel. "And ye shall know that I am in the midst of Israel, and that I am the LORD your God, and none else: and my people shall never be ashamed" (Joel 2:27).

Searching the Scriptures

I. DESCRIPTION OF THE LOCUST PLAGUE

God showed Joel a day to come when the land would be stripped bare, not by human armies with superior strength and innovative technology, but by hordes of common insects. These insects—among the smallest and most primitive of all life-forms—would voraciously eat every plant until nothing was left for humankind, the crown of God's creation and to whom He had given the plants for food.

Joel listed the insects by name: palmerworm, locust, cankerworm, and caterpillar. According to the *Evangelical Commentary on the Bible*, some scholars apply these names to "successive stages in the growth of the immature insect." Thus the meager leftovers of one developing generation would be consumed by the next and the next until nothing was left but bare pastures, withered stalks, and dead tree stumps. Mankind, with his superior intellect and strength, would be powerless to stop the army of devouring insects. The devastation would serve as a powerful lesson to teach the people of Judah the futility of trusting in their own instincts and intellect more than they trusted in God.

The world had never seen a nature-induced famine of this magnitude. It would be of such epic proportions that succeeding generations would tell the story to their children. The devastation would affect everyone.

1. *Vintners.* Those who depended upon the vines to produce the grapes from which they made their wine wept when they found their treasured plants ruined. Those who drank to excess began to howl when their supply was gone and no more could be made because the vines had been stripped.

2. *Priests.* These administrators of the ritual sacrifices—a portion of which became their own—mourned because there was no harvest from which to gather a sacrifice. Even though the priests were the Lord's ministers, they were not spared, but suffered loss with all the families of Judah.

3. *Farmers.* Husbandmen were ashamed because in spite of extreme effort their work was fruitless. The seed they planted rotted in the ground (Joel 1:17). Their cattle and herds dwindled for lack of pasturage. Even the barns were destroyed as hungry men raided the storage bins and there was no corn or grain to refill them.

4. *Waterways.* Rivers dried up causing the wild animals to cry out. The prophet himself cried to the Lord because of the devastation that came upon them (Joel 1:19-20).

II. DESCRIPTION
OF THE ENEMY INVASION

In chapter 2 of his prophecy, Joel described his vision of the largest and strongest army ever to be assembled (Joel 2:2). Before the invasion the beauty and lushness of the land rivaled the Garden of Eden; but this army ravaged it like wildfire raging through a dry forest. Nothing but ash and stubble remained (Joel 2:3).

This vast army was as swift and sure footed as war horses. They swarmed over the land,

never breaking rank and consuming everything in their wake. The scurrying and munching of untold millions of insects shook the earth like rumbling chariots. Their buzzing sounded like the roar of a consuming fire. Their swarms turned the sky inky black and the faces of their victims paled as hopelessness covered them like a shroud. Like warriors trained for battle, the army advanced. No wall could withstand them and no sword could wound them. No house was secure; they entered at will.

When the Lord's patience comes to an end, He sends trials and difficulties, hoping they will cause the individual to turn to Him in repentance.

III. DIVINE APPEAL
TO JUDAH TO REPENT

A. The Lord Calls on People to Repent

In the process of describing the great and terrible day of the Lord, the prophet paused to swing wide the door to the mercy of God. God's people were not left without a way of escape, as Joel told them how to make "the Lord be jealous for his land, and pity his people" (Joel 2:18). Despite the prophet's message of impending doom, it was not too late for Judah to cry out to God in repentance.

> "Gather the people, sanctify the congregation, assemble the elders, gather the children. . . . Let the priests, the ministers of the Lord, weep between the porch and the altar, and let them say, Spare thy people, O Lord, and give not thine heritage to reproach" (Joel 2:16-17).

In the New Testament, Paul echoed these concerns. He rebuked the person who disregards the goodness and forbearance of God, not knowing or caring that these attributes

14

should lead him to repentance. Instead, he presumes upon God's longsuffering and continues in his wicked ways. (See Romans 2:4.) When the Lord's patience comes to an end, He sends trials and difficulties, hoping they will cause the individual to turn to Him in repentance.

"The Lord is not slack concerning his promise, as some men count slackness; but is longsuffering to usward, not willing that any should perish, but that all should come to repentance" (II Peter 3:9).

B. Repentance Must Be More Than Outward Ritual

Genuine repentance is more than a symbolic religious ritual. John the Baptist, the great forerunner of the Messiah, affirmed this when he demanded the Pharisees and Sadducees to "bring forth therefore fruits meet for repentance" (Matthew 3:8). While repentance includes behavioral changes that produce observable actions (which John called fruits), the work must originate within the heart. God said to Judah, "Turn ye even to me with all your heart" (Joel 2:12).

Mankind uses religious ritual in the attempt to enhance his standing before God on his own terms. While religious rituals may resemble true worship on the surface, their underlying motive is to satisfy the whims of the worshiper rather than to bring him into submission to the commandments of God. For this reason God rejected King Saul, telling him that "to obey is better than sacrifice, and to hearken than the fat of rams" (I Samuel 15:22). It is not that God does not desire the sacrifice; but when the ritual is performed without obedience to His Word, those actions cease to be worship.

Transparency / 1

Transparency 1 depicts a plague of locusts and quotes a portion of Joel 2:13.

Joel's appeal to Judah strongly indicated that God desires sincere worship. "And rend your heart, and not your garments, and turn unto the LORD your God: for he is gracious and merciful, slow to anger, and of great kindness, and repenteth him of the evil" (Joel 2:13). God did not desire to see outward signs of Judah's humility such as sackcloth and ashes. He longed for their hearts to hold genuine affection for Him.

Prayer is the tool a person must use to turn his or her heart to God. Sincere prayer begins the transformation and is essential to sustaining any change. Every other spiritual discipline must be accompanied by prayer to be profitable.

The destruction Joel foretold could be countered only by deliberate and strong spiritual action. In our Christian walk prayer alone cannot turn back the attacking forces. Winning this battle requires the active participation and complete submission of every member of the body of Christ. Prayer involves the intellect, but God's call to repentance demands more than just mental agreement. To turn the tide of evil spiritual aggression also requires that our will be broken through fasting, our conscience renewed by mourning, and our heart cleansed through weeping. Nothing short of total commitment moves the heart of God.

Nothing liberates the spirit from the grip of carnality like prayer and fasting.

IV. DECLARATION OF A FAST

Joel's clarion call to Judah is also the church's battle plan for complete spiritual victory. Normal measures and predictable behavior may win an occasional battle, but only passionate obedience to the Word of God will win the war. King Joash's minimal reaction to Elisha's command to strike the ground with a handful of arrows aroused Elisha's wrath. The prophet shouted, "Thou shouldest have smitten five or six times; then hadst thou smitten Syria till thou hadst consumed it" (II Kings 13:19). Complete victory over the enemy requires passionate and committed spiritual warfare.

Joel delivered his message in very few words, but to carry it out required considerable effort. He did not want a handful of people to participate in mere symbolic gestures; he wanted the entire congregation immersed in the process of spiritual renewal. He expected every person, from the nursing infants to the ruling elders, to join in. They were to fast and cleanse themselves, and then present themselves as a united group before their leaders.

15

Sanctification was necessary in order to be set apart for the Lord's service. This process, depending upon a person's circumstances and condition, could span several days. The prescription was the same for all, but each individual had to apply the instructions to his or her personal situation. God's Word, through the Law He gave to Moses, showed them how they could be considered clean in the sight of God.

Fasting is useful in personal cleansing. Nothing liberates the spirit from the grip of carnality like prayer and fasting. The prophet Isaiah said fasting will cause the light to "break forth as the morning, and thine health shall spring forth speedily: and thy righteousness shall go before thee; the glory of the LORD shall be thy rereward. Then shalt thou call, and the LORD shall answer; thou shalt cry, and he shall say, Here I am" (Isaiah 58:8-9).

Once the people had sanctified themselves, they were to assemble as a congregation. When a person follows the prescription for cleansing given by God, it will wash away pride and selfishness and allow the church to come together in unity.

V. DIVINE DELIVERANCE PROMISED

Joel delivered God's call to Judah in plain and concise language that clearly defined the pathway to repentance. With similar clarity, he described how God would respond to His people's prayers.

Dr. Abraham Maslow, one of the founders of humanistic psychology, is credited with being the first to recognize the universality of human needs. He organized those needs into a hierarchical structure that illustrates the order in which those needs must be met in order to sustain physical and mental health. Dr. Maslow theorized the more basic needs must be met before attempting to satisfy higher-level needs. A person's need for food and water, for example, must be satisfied before that individual's educational needs can be addressed.

Dr. Maslow's recent "discovery" has been a biblical principle for centuries. Better than any psychologist's handbook, the Word of God is the complete source of knowledge "because the foolishness of God is wiser than men; and the weakness of God is stronger than men" (I Corinthians 1:25).

Transparency / 2

Transparency 2 shows the heirarchy of needs and quotes Joel 2:26.

God's promises to repentant Judah in the Book of Joel began with meeting their most basic needs and progressing upward until each level of need had been met. First, He sent rain in due season. The pastures sprang up, the trees bore fruit, and the vines yielded their strength. The granaries were stuffed with wheat and storage vats overflowed with wine and oil. They thanked the Lord for His wonderful works. (See Joel 2:21-26.)

God does not view His people as objects of His creation, but He considers them His children. "Like as a father pitieth his children, so the LORD pitieth them that fear him" (Psalm 103:13). God recognizes His children's needs, promises to meet them, and faithfully fulfills His promises.

"Therefore take no thought, saying, What shall we eat? or, What shall we drink? or, Wherewithal shall we be clothed? (For after all these things do the Gentiles seek:) for your heavenly Father knoweth that ye have need of all these things. But seek ye first the kingdom of God, and his righteousness; and all these things shall be added unto you" (Matthew 6:31-33).

Not only does God give us life, but also the ability to sustain life comes from Him.

A. Material Prosperity

Judah's most basic need was to find a source to replace the food that was lost to the devouring locusts. After Judah repented, God's first promise to them was "I will send you corn, and wine, and oil, and ye shall be satisfied therewith" (Joel 2:19). God stated clearly that not only would He provide for their sustenance, but also He would forgive their sins. God wanted Judah to know they owed their very existence to Him.

Not only does God give us life, but also the ability to sustain life comes from Him. Since He is the source of everything that exists, His people can be confident He will supply their needs regardless of how impossible it may seem.

The purpose of God's blessing Judah with material goods was not to make them wealthy, but to ensure they had the means to feed themselves and their children. God designed the human body to require constant nourishment. Without it, the body grows weak and the mind loses its ability to function. By providing food, God ensured that His children who had prepared themselves for His service would have the strength to do so.

As faith grows, fear diminishes.

B. Destruction of the Enemy

God's response to Judah's repentance included the destruction of their enemies. By driving the enemy out of their land, God removed the source of their greatest fear. The need to live in safety follows on the heels of man's need for food and water. God's promise to destroy Judah's enemies established a safe zone in which Judah could dwell and flourish. With the enemy removed, the peace of God could reign unhindered.

When we respond in faith to our Savior, He removes our fears. Since fear opposes faith, the two cannot coexist. Repentance and dependence upon God reduce fear because as faith grows, fear diminishes.

C. Pouring Out of God's Spirit

God never intended simply to provide a good life for His people. He gives material and physical blessings to enhance and empower our spiritual relationship with Him. If Judah would repent, God promised He would provide them with food and peace, which would prepare them to receive the spiritual gift He desired to impart.

The gift of the Holy Spirit is like no other gift God has given to man. This gift is the capstone of the new birth. Further, it empowers individuals to be witnesses (Acts 1:8) and is an integral part of the kingdom of God. (See Romans 14:17.) However, one of the most significant purposes for giving the Holy Ghost is to connect mankind to the very purpose for which he was created. "What? know ye not that your body is the temple of the Holy Ghost which is in you, which ye have of God, and ye are not your own? For ye are bought with a price: therefore glorify God in your body, and in your spirit, which are God's" (I Corinthians 6:19-20). Humans were created to be the dwelling place of the Spirit of God.

God pours out His Spirit not only to endue a person with immediate power, but also to redeem him and to prepare him for the end of time: a time of great turmoil and wonder.

D. Signs Preceding Christ's Second Coming

Joel declared God will show signs in both the heavens and the earth before that great day of the Lord will come (Joel 2:31). The sun will be darkened and the moon will turn to blood, accompanied by fire and columns of smoke. But even in the midst of such horrific events, God will rescue and deliver His people to the place He has prepared for them (Joel 2:32).

E. Judgment of Gentile Nations

Just as God promised to restore to Judah all that the insects had devoured, He promised to gather His children who had been scattered around the world. He also will cause the nations to gather and will judge the heathen from the valley of Jehoshaphat (Joel 3:12).

F. Restoration and Future Blessing of the Jews

Joel concluded his prophecy by reminding all of God's people they are destined to experience restoration and they will continue with the Lord forever.

VI. THE DESCRIPTION OF JOEL'S REVIVAL

Transparency 3

Transparency 3 quotes a portion of Joel 2:28.

A. A Sweeping Revival

Joel's call to repentance included every person. No individual or group was exempt. No one was too important or too insignificant for inclusion. Every age group and every societal class received the same command.

God's call to repentance echoes still. The way into His presence today is the way Joel described to the inhabitants of Judah. If we will repent, rend our hearts, and cleanse ourselves as His Word commands, we will find the same acceptance He promised to Judah.

No man or woman is exempt; we all must come to God the same way. His call is universal. "Behold, I stand at the door, and knock: if any man hear my voice, and open the door, I will come in to him, and will sup with him, and he with me" (Revelation 3:20).

B. A Weeping Revival

We cannot accomplish the repentance necessary to move the heart of God by performing mere rituals. The impetus for change must come from a heart that is broken because of trespass and error, and that is determined to set things right. This kind of repentance goes much deeper than a mental decision, but it affects the emotions as well. It compels a person to fast, to cleanse his ways, and to humble himself in obedience to the Word of God.

C. A Reaping Revival

If Judah responded as Joel instructed, then God promised He would rekindle His concern for His people and His land and He would seal their deliverance. Not only would He save Judah, but He would meet their basic needs and align His people with God's eternal purpose for their nation.

As we repent and submit our lives to God's Word, we become connected to His purpose for our individual lives and for the corporate body of the church as well. Just as He promised Judah, He will sustain us, grant us His peace, and fill us with His empowering Spirit.

Internalizing the Message

God leaves nothing to chance. He calls us to walk by faith; but that faith is more often demonstrated by our obedience to His Word than it is by our clinging to His hand when we cannot find our own way. In Joel's prophecy, we find the gateway to God's presence and favor—if we sincerely desire it. He does not leave the lost and hungry soul to wander aimlessly; He established the pattern long ago, and the cost is the same for every individual.

Prayer is the gateway into the presence of God. Fasting brings victory over our carnal nature. Submission to God's Word washes and sanctifies our soul and sets us apart for service unto the Lord.

God pronounces a special blessing upon those who repent, rend their hearts, and cleanse themselves for His service: "And I will restore to you the years that the locust hath eaten, the cankerworm, and the caterpiller, and the palmerworm, my great army which I sent among you. And ye shall eat in plenty, and be satisfied, and praise the name of the LORD your God, that hath dealt wondrously with you: and my people shall never be ashamed" (Joel 2:25-26).

REFLECTIONS

- Prayer is the gateway into the presence of God. Discuss.
- God sent dire circumstances to the people of Judah to turn their hearts back to Him. Apply this principle to the Christian life today and discuss reasons why punishment can also involve mercy.
- The process of sanctification sets us apart for God's service. Discuss the steps toward sanctification.
- Individual repentance produces corporate unity. Discuss.
- Discuss the ways in which rituals and traditions can interfere with sincere worship.

Amos— the Lion's Roar

3 week of 06.16.13

Lesson Text

Amos 1:1, 3-4, 6-7, 9-10, 13-15

1 The words of Amos, who was among the herdmen of Tekoa, which he saw concerning Israel in the days of Uzziah king of Judah, and in the days of Jeroboam the son of Joash king of Israel, two years before the earthquake.

. . . . .

3 Thus saith the LORD; For three transgressions of Damascus, and for four, I will not turn away the punishment thereof; because they have threshed Gilead with threshing instruments of iron:
4 But I will send a fire into the house of Hazael, which shall devour the palaces of Ben-hadad.

. . . . .

6 Thus saith the LORD; For three transgressions of Gaza, and for four, I will not turn away the punishment thereof; because they carried away captive the whole captivity, to deliver them up to Edom:
7 But I will send a fire on the wall of Gaza, which shall devour the palaces thereof:

. . . . .

9 Thus saith the LORD; For three transgressions of Tyrus, and for four, I will not turn away the punishment thereof; because they delivered up the whole captivity to Edom, and remembered not the brotherly covenant:
10 But I will send a fire on the wall of Tyrus, which shall devour the palaces thereof.

. . . . .

13 Thus saith the LORD; For three transgressions of the children of Ammon, and for four, I will not turn away the punishment thereof; because they have ripped up the women with child of Gilead, that they might enlarge their border:
14 But I will kindle a fire in the wall of Rabbah, and it shall devour the palaces thereof, with shouting in the day of battle, with a tempest in the day of the whirlwind:
15 And their king shall go into captivity, he and his princes together, saith the LORD.

Focus Thought

God will roar out judgment against all who live contrary to His will.

Focus Verse

Amos 1:2
And he said, The LORD will roar from Zion, and utter his voice from Jerusalem; and the habitations of the shepherds shall mourn, and the top of Carmel shall wither.

19

Punishing the Sinner and Growing the Believer

by Gary D. Erickson

The judgments of God are under the control of His sovereign purposes. They are certain but can be difficult to identify. Some believe New Orleans was flooded by Katrina because of the sins of the city. Could it have been because the city planners did not prepare the levies, pumps, and canal network properly for the inevitable massive hurricane? Others believe the World Trade Center was destroyed because of America's sins. Could it have been only the vengeful activity of evil terrorists? Some people are quick to pronounce God's judgment upon bad people when they are sick or suffer loss. What do we call it when believers suffer sickness and loss? Quickly declaring that tragic events are God's judgment can get us into trouble and make us look foolish.

God sends judgment to punish the wicked as this lesson confirms (Romans 2:9). Nevertheless, He also sends pain and suffering to believers to make them grow spiritually (Romans 5:3-4). Sometimes God tests a person's faith and develops character with pain. Even Jesus learned obedience through the things He suffered (Hebrews 5:8).

When tragedy befalls believers, it works in tandem with all other things in their lives to accomplish good. Paul said, "And we know that all things work together for good to them that love God, to them who are the called according to his purpose" (Romans 8:28). It may rain on the just and the unjust (Matthew 5:45), but the purpose achieved differs. God disciplines the righteous, but He punishes the wicked. The same tragic event can be punishment for the sinner and an opportunity for growth for the believer. Our status with God makes the difference.

I. GOD—THE LION—ROARS OUT THREATS OF JUDGMENTS ON EIGHT NATIONS
II. THE GUILT AND PUNISHMENT OF ISRAEL
III. THE SYMBOLS OF APPROACHING JUDGMENT
  A. The Plague of Locusts
  B. The Devouring Fire
  C. The Plumbline
  D. Refusal of Amos to Be Intimidated
  E. The Basket of Summer Fruit
  F. The Striking of the Lintel
IV. THE FUTURE RESTORATION OF ISRAEL
V. GOD WILL ROAR OUT JUDGMENT FOR ALL WHO LIVE CONTRARY TO HIS WILL
  A. Everyone Will Have to Stand Judgment
  B. The Final Judgment on Sin and Sinners

Contemplating the Topic

The biographical details for the life of Amos exist only in what he shared in his writing. There is no corroboration or supporting evidence for these details. He told us he was not a prophet, priest, or religious professional. Instead, he earned his living as a shepherd. According to C. Hassell Bullock, his flocks may have been a breed of short-legged sheep that produced very fine wool (*An Introduction to the Old Testament Prophetic Books*, 1977). Amos also was a "gatherer of sycamore fruit" (Amos 7:14).

After the desert pastures had dried up in late summer, the shepherds of Tekoa would lead their flocks to western Judah where the grass was still green. Fig trees grew in this area, so landowners would trade grazing rights for labor. The sycamore fig was smaller than the common fig; and since it did not taste as sweet, it generally was eaten by the poor people. Nonetheless, it needed to be pinched or pierced about four days before harvesting so it would ripen completely.

Amos did not claim to be a prophet or the son of a prophet. But clearly there was more to Amos than sheep and figs. He could speak well and write well, especially when anointed by the Spirit of God. By divine compulsion he left his flocks behind, crossed the border into Israel, and began to preach at Bethel, one of the centers of the corrupt state religion established by Jeroboam.

No one had ever seen Amos so stirred up. They had never witnessed such a ferocious manner and tone. He roared out God's message like a lion—and God was the lion.

I. GOD—THE LION—ROARS OUT THREATS OF JUDGMENT ON EIGHT NATIONS

Transparency 1

Transparency 1 says, "The Lord will roar from Zion, and utter his voice from Jerusalem" (Amos 1:2).

Humanity is always reaching for improvement, growth, and profit. We organize, prepare, and plan for better days and times, but catastrophe can strike suddenly and swiftly. Consider the earthquakes, hurricanes, and other natural disasters that strike our world so unexpectedly and ruthlessly and with devastating consequences. The total impact often requires days and weeks to assess. Some would say these are the judgments of God; some say they are merely acts of nature; and some do not know what to think. Regardless of how we categorize the events, the results are dire, the presentation violent, and the effects long lasting. The lull before the storm deceives many into apathy, contentment, and delusion.

Amos began preaching in Bethel, the first city of consequence across Israel's border from Judah. His Israelite audience must have agreed with the fiery preacher and "egged him on" as he castigated the six surrounding nations for their crimes: Damascus, Gaza, Tyre, Edom, Ammon, and Moab. He prophesied God would send a fire to devour the citadels and cut off the inhabitants; however, these foreign nations were not present to hear the message of judgment. They had not enjoyed the covenant privileges and responsibilities of the people of God. But they had a basic knowledge of the ethical demands of God through general revelation and were therefore accountable.

In chapter 2 Amos transitioned to an accusation against the southern kingdom of Judah for its backsliding and then suddenly turned the tables on his audience and indicted Israel.

II. THE GUILT AND PUNISHMENT OF ISRAEL

In chapters 3 through 6 Amos turned God's judgment on Israel. The declarative "You only have I known of all the families of the earth" (Amos 3:2) expressed a special relationship that became a call for punishment. Spiritual insight and blessing not only bring privilege but also bring responsibility. God's faithfulness to the covenant with Abraham hinged upon the family of Abraham blessing all the earth.

"Get thee out of thy country, and from thy kindred, and from thy father's house, unto a land that I will shew thee: and I will make of thee a great nation, and I will bless thee, and make thy name great; and thou shalt be a blessing: and I will bless them that bless thee, and curse him that curseth thee: and in thee shall all families of the earth be blessed" (Genesis 12:1-3).

This requirement to be a bestower of blessings was Israel's responsibility, not the nation's status. Mistaking their unique position as status was one of the errors Israel repeated throughout its history. Jesus contended with it in the Sadducees and Pharisees. Their sins of social injustice, immoral exemptions, and power-hungry greed turned them into a "bless me" community rather than a "giving" community. Giving that is self-serving and self-perpetuating is not charity. God desires that His people make a global impact—not for personal glory but so the world can be saved.

Spiritual insight and blessing not only bring privilege but also bring responsibility.

Amos 3:10 elaborated on this dilemma: "For they know not to do right . . . who store up violence and robbery in their palaces." The sense of personal gain from divine appointment had corrupted the populace. When Amos recounted the blessings of God for His people in chapter 2, he listed a series of interventions and deliverances for all of Israel, not for individuals or certain segments. There was no special intervention for priests or kings. There was no particular blessing to a merchant or a shepherd. God's interventions were for God's people as a whole. Too many times in the decision between right and wrong an individual will insert the question, "What is right for me?" God hates this self-serving error. He would have us ask, "What is right for the people of God?"

III. THE SYMBOLS OF APPROACHING JUDGMENT

A. The Plague of Locusts

Amos saw a vision of a cloud of locusts poised to descend on Israel (Amos 7:1). Locust plagues were a natural phenomenon and a part of Israel's history. In times of Israel's backslidings, God used locust plagues as a call to repent, but lamented, "Yet have ye not returned unto me" (Amos 4:9). Worried about Israel's survival, Amos stepped away from his role as the foreteller of judgment and into the role of an intercessor. He prayed, "O Lord GOD forgive, I beseech thee: by whom shall Jacob arise? for he is small" (Amos 7:2). Amos's intercessory prayer touched the heart of God and He did not send the locust plague.

B. The Devouring Fire

Amos foresaw a great fire consuming Israel. In Israel's dry season the fire would spread rapidly, drying up rivers and creek beds and destroying vegetation, people, and entire villages. Fearful for Israel's total annihilation, Amos again pleaded with God to stay the punishment, and God relented.

It is important to note God's "repentance" (Amos 7:3, 6) did not imply any regret or remorse on His part for His intention to send these first two judgments. Instead, His "repentance" underlined His personal involvement in the affairs of His people, and that He held them accountable for their actions. Despite His love for Israel, He would not automatically forgive their sins without sufficient evidence of true repentance. Further, God's repentance indicated complete annihilation was not His plan for Israel's salvation; He would preserve a remnant. (See Amos 9:8.)

C. The Plumbline

A plumbline is a string with a weight tied to one end. A workman stands on a ladder and dangles the line until it establishes a straight line against which a straight wall can be built.

Transparency 2 shows a plumbline and quotes a portion of Amos 7:8.

Amos's vision of a plumbline was not one of an external destructive force such as a locust plague or a fire. He saw God holding a plumbline (God's law) against Israel's "crooked" behavior. (See Amos 7:7-9.) God had originally planned that His people would exemplify His holiness to the pagan nations; instead, Israel had persisted in conforming to the vile practices of their neighbors. Israel's multitude of transgressions against God's law made their wall reel like a drunken man till it threatened to topple the entire structure. Israel would bring down destruction on her own head.

D. Refusal of Amos to Be Intimidated

The passage in Amos 7:10-17 provides a detailed account of a hostile encounter between Amos and Amaziah, the chief priest at Bethel. Bethel was a center of Israel's religious cult and the seat of a shrine dedicated to the golden calf made by Jeroboam I. Amaziah elbowed Amos aside and charged him with treason. The priest hurriedly dispatched a messenger to King Jeroboam II with the message that Amos had predicted Jeroboam's death. Amaziah turned back to Amos and sneered, "You call yourself a prophet. Take your so-called prophecies back where you came from and don't show your face here again!" Amos countered, "I never claimed to be a prophet. I was a herdsman and gatherer of sycamore fruit until God called me and sent me here with a message for His people Israel."

Amaziah had not expected a direct confrontation from this obviously rustic rabble-rouser. He must have recoiled in deep shock when Amos looked him in the eye and roared, "Hear the word of the Lord!" Then he pronounced defilement, degradation, and death upon the house of Amaziah.

E. The Basket of Summer Fruit

Chapter 8 gives a vivid account of Amos's vision of a basket of delicious, ripe fruit. According to *Zondervan Bible Commentary*, "The point of the vision depends on a play on words in the Hebrew. The basket of ripe fruit (*qayiits*) reminds Amos not of the joyful harvest festival but that Israel is ripe for judgment and the time (*qets*) is ripe." During the coming Assyrian invasion, depicted like an overwhelming flood, dead bodies would be flung out like overripe fruit. It was as if God were saying, "I've had enough. You've crossed the line from forbearance into judgment."

F. The Striking of the Lintel

Amos said, "I saw the Lord standing upon the altar" (9:1). An individual's first impression might be that God intended to bless His people with His presence. Instead, God said, "Smite the lintel of the door." Destruction would begin at the altar and cut down "all of them." No one would be able to escape even on the highest point on earth or at the bottom of the sea.

Yet, after this most devastating vision, God assured Amos He would "not utterly destroy the house of Jacob" (9:8), but would preserve a remnant and someday raise up the fallen Tabernacle of David. The promised future restoration would reverse the punishment God was about to bring upon Israel.

God is a God of mercy but also of judgment. He bestows mercy on those who come to Him with contrite hearts, weeping, and repentance. He also expresses mercy in warnings of future judgment. Like a lumberjack yelling "Timber!" before the tree falls, prophets sounded the alarm of coming destruction. After God sent Amos to shout a warning, He gave Israel space to repent. Approximately thirty years elapsed from Amos's prophecy until the Assyrian invasion of Israel.

> *God is a God of mercy but also of judgment.*

IV. THE FUTURE RESTORATION OF ISRAEL

Woven into the prophecies of gloom and doom we see a thread of hope. In the last five verses of the Book of Amos, God's longsuffering produced a hope of restoration. Like the glorious dawn after a stormy night, the utter destruction of Israel transitioned to a new "day" (Amos 9:11) wherein the tabernacle was foreseen as being restored. This tabernacle was not Solomon's magnificent Temple but the temporary dwelling of the Ark of the Covenant David erected when he brought the Ark back to Jerusalem. (See II Samuel 6:17.) The tabernacle of David was his dynasty, which God promised would be "established for ever before thee; thy throne shall be established for ever" (II Samuel 7:16).

God would restore the united kingdom and "plant" His people in the Promised Land, "and they shall no more be pulled up out of their land which I have given them, saith the LORD thy God" (Amos 9:15). Then the authority of their Messiah would extend to all nations. God's people would enjoy unprecedented productivity, indicated by Amos 9:13 where he described the land "in terms of the garden of Eden" (*Evangelical Commentary on the Bible*). Their long sojourn in Babylon had taught this remnant of backsliding people that the terms of their covenant with God involved obligations, responsibilities, and obedience. At last, Israel's wholehearted love and service to God would become a temple in which God would dwell permanently.

> *"The place of my throne, and the place of the soles of my feet, where I will dwell in the midst of the children of Israel for ever, and my holy name, shall the house of Israel no more defile" (Ezekiel 43:7).*

V. GOD WILL ROAR OUT JUDGMENT FOR ALL WHO LIVE CONTRARY TO HIS WILL

A. Everyone Will Have to Stand Judgment

Transparency 3

Transparency 3 quotes Ecclesiastes 12:14.

Amos helps us to understand that all will be judged by the same standard, both the heathen and the people of God. The Book of Revelation describes more fully the future judgment for all nations pronounced by Amos. "The dead, small and great, stand before God." Death and Hell and the sea will give up their dead, and they shall be "judged every man according to their works" (Revelation 20:12).

It is clear that the dead will stand at the Great White Throne judgment. However, instead of facing God at the Great White Throne judgment, the people of God are judged at "the judgment seat of Christ: that

23

every one may receive the things done in his body, according to that he hath done, whether it be good or bad" (II Corinthians 5:10). I Thessalonians 4:16-17 reveals that the dead in Christ and "we which are alive and remain," having already been judged, will be "caught up . . . in the clouds, to meet the Lord in the air: and so shall we ever be with the Lord."

Amos's message was the same: everyone will face God at the judgment. "The day of the LORD is darkness, and not light" (Amos 5:18). It will be a terrifying day. Paul wrote, "Knowing therefore the terror of the Lord, we persuade men" (II Corinthians 5:11). Knowing the terrible vengeance God will mete out upon the workers of iniquity, it behooves every believer to use every means of persuasion to lead others to believe on the Lord Jesus and become His disciples.

B. The Final Judgment on Sin and Sinners

The awesome specter of eternity is both glorious and terrible. Our lives will be divinely assessed according to our deeds, and God will send us into everlasting light or everlasting darkness. The descriptions of these two opposite destinations are woefully inadequate, for John had to use earthly perception and words when depicting otherworldly places and consequences. Our minds cannot comprehend what these options and their consequences really mean for us individually.

For the redeemed, trying to imagine no sea (Revelation 21:1), no tears or death (Revelation 21: 4), and no need of sun or moon (Revelation 21:23) only begins to underscore what the writer meant by "all things new" (Revelation 21:5). Our glorious destination will forever fill our being with light, for the glory of God will lighten it. (See Revelation: 21:23.)

Likewise, the Revelator's description of the "lake of fire" cannot convey to us the horror and anguish of those who are cast into the fire (Revelation 19:20; 20:10, 14) to be tormented forever in the presence of Satan, the fallen angels (Jude 6), the Antichrist, and the false prophet. They will exist in "outer darkness" (Matthew 22:13; 25:30), separated forever from the presence and mercy of God.

The Word of God is the standard by which all the souls who have ever lived will be judged. His Word warns His adversaries about impending "judgment and fiery indignation" (Hebrews 10:27). His mercy fills sinners with fearful foreboding that they will someday face Him in judgment and will be unable to escape. (See Hebrews 10:27.) Yet His mercy will not let Him send swift, fiery judgment without giving the sinner space to repent.

Internalizing the Message

"Neither is there any creature that is not manifest in his sight: but all things are naked and opened unto the eyes of him with whom we have to do" (Hebrews 4:13).

The *New International Version* renders Hebrews 4:13: "Nothing in all creation is hidden from God's sight. Everything is uncovered and laid bare before the eyes of him to whom we must give account." God warns that judgment is coming to all. His Word names the good actions that will be rewarded and the bad actions that will reap judgment. His mercy gives us time to compare our deeds, not to the world's standards, but to the plumbline in His Word, and to repent of any wrongdoing.

"For the Lord himself shall descend from heaven with a shout, with the voice of the archangel, and with the trump of God: and the dead in Christ shall rise first: then we which are alive and remain shall be caught up together with them in the clouds, to meet the Lord in the air: and so shall we ever be with the Lord" (I Thessalonians 4:16-17).

Amos delivered God's indictment against the heathen nations, against Judah, and against Israel. Amos's message identified the sins of God's people and promised He would surely judge them if they did not repent.

Like self-satisfied Israel, we may look at society and think the sins of other people are much worse than the sins we have committed. There is rampant abortion, homosexuality, murder, lust, envy, abuse—the list is endless. We have seen in Amos that God is aware of the sins of the "heathen," and they surely will be judged if they do not repent.

But we should not fall into the trap of judging ourselves better than the world just because our sins seem so much "smaller" than their "big" sins. In reality, we do things that are, in God's eyes, worse, because we know better. Just as God expected more of His people Israel, He expects more of His people today. We dare not gloss over what we think are little sins, or appease our conscience by this type of rationalization.

God pronounced coming judgment on the eight surrounding nations, "for three transgressions . . . and for four"—or their many transgressions. However, He did not list them. But when it came to Israel's transgressions, He compiled a long list of indictments.

- Rank materialism
- Stiff-necked pleasure seekers
- Love of luxury; self-indulgence
- Drunkenness
- Dishonest judges; corrupt government
- Bribery
- Extortion
- Immorality
- Superstition
- Self-deception
- Businessmen getting rich while oppressing the poor
- Class hatred
- Feuds
- Broken covenants
- Outward show of religion

Why did God seem to judge Israel more harshly than He did the heathen nations? He judged Israel more harshly because of the biblical principle "the greater the privilege, the greater the responsibility." God had given much to Israel: a Promised Land, provision, victory over their enemies, prosperity, and so on. He had revealed Himself to them through the Law and made a covenant with them.

God has also given us much: His Word, His Son, His promises, provision, fellowship with Him and the body of Christ, the Holy Ghost, His name . . . the list is endless. He also gave us the example of Israel and expects us to learn from Israel's mistakes. Through the written Word and the preached Word He gives us guidelines on how we ought to behave ourselves. When He convicts us of wrongdoing, He gives us space to repent. If we do not repent, we will reap harsh punishment upon ourselves.

God is a God of righteous judgment. Amos taught us to view God's judgment in a positive light, not a negative light. For if we do well, we have nothing to fear.

"Let judgment run down as waters, and righteousness as a mighty stream" (Amos 5:24).

REFLECTIONS

- God's judgments are well deserved. He does not mete out judgment without first sending a warning. Discuss.
- God judges the saved and the unsaved by the same standard. Discuss.
- Arguably, Israel's greatest sin was self-deception. We can deceive ourselves until God finally sends a strong delusion. (See II Thessalonians 2:11.) Discuss.
- Israel's bad example teaches us that along with privileges comes responsibility. Discuss.
- It is not wise to compare our own sins with the sins of others. Discuss.

4
week of
06.23.13

Obadiah—
Restoration and Revival

Lesson Text

Obadiah 15-21

15 For the day of the LORD is near upon all the heathen: as thou hast done, it shall be done unto thee: thy reward shall return upon thine own head.

16 For as ye have drunk upon my holy mountain, so shall all the heathen drink continually, yea, they shall drink, and they shall swallow down, and they shall be as though they had not been.

17 But upon mount Zion shall be deliverance, and there shall be holiness; and the house of Jacob shall possess their possessions.

18 And the house of Jacob shall be a fire, and the house of Joseph a flame, and the house of Esau for stubble, and they shall kindle in them, and devour them; and there shall not be any remaining of the house of Esau; for the LORD hath spoken it.

19 And they of the south shall possess the mount of Esau; and they of the plain the Philistines: and they shall possess the fields of Ephraim, and the fields of Samaria: and Benjamin shall possess Gilead.

20 And the captivity of this host of the children of Israel shall possess that of the Canaanites, even unto Zarephath; and the captivity of Jerusalem, which is in Sepharad, shall possess the cities of the south.

21 And saviours shall come up on mount Zion to judge the mount of Esau; and the kingdom shall be the LORD'S.

Focus Thought

God promises His people that even though they stray far from Him, He will restore and revive them if they repent.

Focus Verse

Obadiah 21

And saviours shall come up on mount Zion to judge the mount of Esau; and the kingdom shall be the LORD'S.

The Hope of Restoration

by Gary D. Erickson

Restoration is the theme of the entire Bible. From the Fall in the Garden of Eden to the unfolding of a future climax, restoration is the prevailing hope. Humankind fell from a lofty place of perfection and intimate fellowship with God to a corrupted state of death, suffering, curses, and separation from God. The Fall was an enormously destructive epoch. In a moment, humanity went from the epitome of perfection and tranquility to corruption and chaos. Adam and Eve were cast from the tranquil garden and made to work under the heat of the sun. They were made to eke out a life in a contrary world. After that precipitous Fall, God began a process of restoration.

A man told me once that he thought the Bible was a sad book. It is certainly filled with many sad events, but it is also filled with hope, abundant hope. Although the Old Testament prophets warned the Hebrews with scathing rebukes and pronouncements of judgment, they always ended with a promise of hope for the righteous. Restoration is the prevailing goal of redemption. The humiliation and ignoble death of Jesus was not only full payment for the price of sin, but it was the apex of the redemptive process.

Jesus rose from the dead and ascended to Heaven to ultimately be exalted as the King of kings and Lord of lords (Ephesians 4:8-10). We see the principle in nature's cycle of life. Life forms die and decay so they may provide fertile nutrients for restoration. The seed dies before it can live again (John 12:24). The new birth through Jesus Christ gives us hope for full restoration.

I. EDOM'S PRIDE TO BE ABASED
II. DESTRUCTION OF EDOM
  A. Completeness of the Plunder
  B. Betrayal by Edom's Allies
  C. Destruction of Edom's Leaders
III. REASONS FOR EDOM'S DOWNFALL
  A. What Edom Did
  B. Edom's Final Doom
IV. EDOM'S JUDGMENT IS RETRIBUTIVE
V. RESTORATION OF ISRAEL AND JUDAH AND EXTINCTION OF EDOM
  A. Edom Is Completely Eradicated
  B. Israel Is Restored and Revived
  C. God Will Visit His People with Restoration and Revival

Contemplating the Topic

It was November 19, 1863, at the dedication of the Soldiers' National Cemetery in Gettysburg, Pennsylvania. The South had surrendered at the Battle of Gettysburg four and one-half months earlier. President Lincoln sat for two hours on a small, makeshift platform waiting for Edward Everett to finish his "eloquent bombast." The president later commented to a reporter, "Now, do you know, I think Edward Everett was very much overrated. He hasn't left any enduring monument."

Lincoln had spent two weeks writing his dedicatory speech; but when Everett finally yielded the floor, it took the president only a little more than two minutes to deliver his speech. He said the issue of slavery had tested the nation's ability to survive; now America must give meaning to the years of tremendous struggle and lead the world to "a new birth of freedom." This brief address, delivered in an unpretentious manner, came to be regarded as one of the greatest speeches in American history (Philip B. Kunhardt et al., *Lincoln: An Illustrated Biography*, New York: Portland House, 1992).

Tucked between the prophecies of Amos and Jonah is the Book of Obadiah. A person can read aloud its twenty-one verses in just over three minutes. Yet, the message of Obadiah had a profound impact on Edom and Judah, and it also can be profitable for the church today.

Obadiah wrote much of his book in the style of a funeral dirge, predicting the death and destruction of Edom for their crimes against their "brother" Jacob. Edom considered Jacob an enemy, which placed the Edomites on God's list of foes. The prophet Nahum wrote, "God is jealous . . . and is furious; the LORD will take vengeance on his adversaries" (Nahum 1:2). It is doubtful Obadiah sealed his letter and sent it from Judah across the border to Edom, so the prophet's intention was not to warn Edom about the judgment he saw looming on the horizon. Instead, the Lord revealed

His plan for Edom's destruction to comfort and encourage the Jews in Babylonian captivity who were still smarting from the violence and treachery perpetrated on them by Edom during Nebuchadnezzar's ruthless campaign against Judah.

Located in an almost inaccessible area of crags, canyons, and rocky extrusions, Edom felt invincible and therefore much more powerful than the nation actually was. But God had no trouble penetrating their defenses. Even the capital city of Sela could not hide from Him. God unleashed His vengeance on Edom when the time was ripe.

Transparency 1

Transparency 1 pictures an eagle and quotes Obadiah 4.

"Though thou exalt thyself as the eagle, and though thou set thy nest among the stars, thence will I bring thee down, saith the LORD" (Obadiah 4).

Searching the Scriptures

I. EDOM'S PRIDE TO BE ABASED

Pride distorts reality and conceals the truth. Pride causes an individual to have an inflated opinion of himself and leads to faulty decisions and actions. In verse 3 Obadiah described God's attitude toward the pride of Edom: "The pride of thine heart hath deceived thee." God does not overlook sinful pride.

Numerous times Solomon warned of the overwhelming danger of pride and the sin it promotes. "Pride goeth before destruction, and an haughty spirit before a fall. Better it is to be of an humble spirit with the lowly, than to divide the spoil with the proud" (Proverbs 16:18-19). Man often deceives himself. For example, many people delude themselves into believing they are saved, yet they manifest no semblance of godliness. They think mere belief in the existence of God makes them "religious" and saves them.

Obadiah warned Edom that God would bring them down (verse 4). Edom was like the eagle that lives in high, unreachable places. From his lofty perch the eagle surveys the world and exalts himself above everyone and everything. The Edomites thought that not even God could bring them down, but they were wrong.

The Lord declared, "Thence I will bring thee down. . . . [Edom] shall be as though they had not been" (verses 4, 16). Edom had snapped the tether of God's mercy and would have to bear the responsibility for their own annihilation. Unlike the house of Jacob, not even a remnant would survive the destruction God would visit upon them.

II. DESTRUCTION OF EDOM

A. Completeness of the Plunder

Obadiah 5-6 points out that if a thief enters a home, he does not take every item in the house. He takes only those things he can either sell or use himself. But such selectivity would not be the case when God punished Edom. It would be as if the thieves came and stole *everything*—to the bare walls. God would ransack the place, ferreting out every hidden treasure and leaving nothing. Edom could blame no one but themselves. "Thy reward shall return upon thine own head" (verse 15). (See also Exodus 21:24-25; Leviticus 24:20; Deuteronomy 19:21.)

B. Betrayal by Edom's Allies

There is often a thin line between a friend and an enemy. The Edomites prided themselves on their vast network of political and economic unions with other countries. But for all of the nation's wisdom, Edom was no more adept at making wise decisions than its ancestor Esau.

Esau had traded the birthright he despised for a bowl of Jacob's pottage. (See Genesis 25:30-33.) When the twins' father, Isaac, grew old and blind, Jacob tricked his father and stole from Esau the material blessing Esau had coveted above all else. He cried bitterly at the loss and vowed to murder his brother. Since that time animosity had seethed between the two "brother" nations.

Obadiah warned Edom the time was ripe for God to avenge Judah for the treachery and abuse perpetrated upon them by Edom, and he even revealed God's instrument of destruction—the allies Edom had trusted.

"The men who were at peace with thee have deceived thee, and prevailed against thee" (Obadiah 7).

Edom's allies laid a trap. They pursued Edom "to the border" and then fled backward, leaving them unprotected and vulnerable.

28

C. Destruction of Edom's Leaders

Teman, located geographically in the southern half of the nation and named after the grandson of Esau, was the center of wisdom and learning in Edom. Jeremiah wrote, "Concerning Edom, . . . Is wisdom no more in Teman? is counsel perished from the prudent? is their wisdom vanished?" (Jeremiah 49:7). (See Obadiah 9.) Edom's leadership was neither wise nor prudent; instead, they were foolish and unscrupulous.

Obadiah indicted Edom's leaders for their role in Jacob's afflictions. While Jacob's enemies were tearing up the land and ravaging the people, Edom's leaders had stood aside, laughing at their brother's calamity. Pleasing the Babylonians mattered more to them than pleasing God. As Jacob was being led away captive, the leaders of Edom encouraged the people to invade their brothers' cities and plunder their substance. The final stroke of treachery came when Edom "stood in the crossway" (verse 14), ambushing Jewish escapees and turning them over to the Babylonians. God's judgment on the leaders of Edom would be swift and fatal.

This speaks to us today of the awesome responsibility of leadership in the twenty-first-century church. Our world, like the helpless children following the Pied Piper of Hamelin, is being led toward certain destruction by foolish and unscrupulous leaders. Believers should thank God for wise spiritual leaders who exercise good judgment and godly wisdom. If we follow them, they will lead us not to a place of destruction, but to a glorious eternal home.

> *Pride causes an individual to have an inflated opinion of himself and leads to faulty decisions and actions.*

III. REASONS FOR EDOM'S DOWNFALL

Obadiah did not mention Edom's priests, temples, or religion. Apparently this nation had no religious base. They were profane like their forefather Esau. The word *profane* used to describe Esau in Hebrews 12:16 means "heathenish" or "wicked." In Romans 9:13 we read that God "hated" Esau and "loved" Jacob; He favored Jacob for his desire for spiritual things and rejected Esau for his sacrilege. Esau's profanity was a disposition that kept surfacing throughout generations of his descendents.

Transparency 2

Transparency 2 lists four reasons for Edom's downfall.

1. *Pride of Wealth.* The Edomites trusted in the wealth they had accumulated by collecting tolls from every caravan that travelled within their boundaries. They trusted in their wealth, for they boasted, "Who shall bring [us] down to the ground?" (Obadiah 3). Sometimes we too trust in things like healthy bank balances or IRAs, but the false sense of security we derive from wealth can be jerked out from under our feet.

Job lost everything in one tragic day, but thankfully he had not placed his trust in his immense wealth but in God. He said, "The LORD gave, and the LORD hath taken away; blessed be the name of the LORD" (Job 1:21). We too should place our trust in God and acknowledge Him as the true source of wealth, both spiritual and material.

2. *Dependence on Ungodly Alliances.* Sometimes allies are not what they seem. Edom's allies, the Moabites and Ammonites, played along until they reached the limits of their so-called friendship—then they, according to one translation, forced Edom from their homeland. Edom's own confederates set an ambush and took them by surprise.

Sometimes people in whom we trust let us down, betray us, and leave us alone when we need them most. For example, new converts are vulnerable to the influence of their worldly friends. Circumstances can quickly become desperate when their friends deceive them and bring them to the very border of destruction. We as Christians should recognize that God is our best friend and ask Him for wisdom to choose our friends wisely.

> In Shakespearean literature, a famous passage warns Julius Caesar to "beware the Ides of March." The speaker was attempting to warn Caesar his friends were not really his friends. His own self-confidence and ego caused him to overlook the warning, and thus he forfeited his life.

3. *Reliance upon Unscrupulous Leaders.* The Scriptures acknowledge there were men of wisdom in Edom (Obadiah 8). Possibly these men had good educations and political astuteness, but obviously they were not wise enough or influential enough to steer Edom away from making many mistakes. These men sacrificed themselves and their countrymen on the altar of ego, and Teman was "cut off by slaughter." Rather than placing blind trust in people whom we think of as wise, we should consult God's Word to learn who is truly wise and follow them as they follow Jesus Christ.

4. *Trusting in Nature and the Military.* The land of Edom had some of the most rugged terrain in the Middle East. It was an immense maze of richly colored mountains, cliffs, chasms, rocky shelves, narrow valleys, and gorges. It also had plateaus, shady basins and sunny headlands. In short, it provided an ideal setting for a fortress of trade and commerce. Due to the ideal terrain, even a small army could defend itself against virtually any foe.

The prophet Obadiah warned, "Thou that dwellest in the clefts of the rock . . . thence will I bring thee down" (Obadiah 3-4). The people of Edom had convinced themselves not even the hand of God, who created the very mountains and clefts they trusted in, could bring them down. Their vain conceit would not let them acknowledge God's deity and power.

A. What Edom Did

Scoffing at another person's afflictions is reprehensible. But abetting the misfortunes of another person, especially a relative, is malicious and hateful. In 586 BC, Nebuchadnezzar's troops swarmed over Judah, slaughtering, pillaging, destroying, and burning. They dismantled Solomon's Temple and plundered the gold and other valuable materials. They took thousands of captives back to Babylon. Edom, Jacob's "brother," should have helped the Jewish refugees who fled across the border for safety, but instead they captured them and handed them over to the Babylonians.

B. Edom's Final Doom

The picture drawn here is one of an utterly cold and heartless lack of restraint in Edom's cruel treatment of God's people. Edom showed no mercy and expended not one shred of compassion on their brothers. Perhaps this betrayal of fraternal relationship sealed their doom. They would have no second chance to redeem themselves and escape total eradication.

Many people depend on a second chance to make things right. Pastors and evangelists commonly hear sinners say "someday" or "maybe next time" as a response to salvation invitations. Like some sinners, Edom waited until it was too late. Jeremiah wrote, "As in the overthrow of Sodom and Gomorrah and the neighbour cities thereof, saith the LORD, no man shall abide there [in Edom], neither shall a son of man dwell in it" (Jeremiah 49:18).

IV. EDOM'S JUDGMENT IS RETRIBUTIVE

"As thou hast done, it shall be done unto thee: thy reward shall return upon thine own head . . . and they shall be as though they had not been" (Obadiah 15-16).

Because of Edom's callous behavior, God vowed they should suffer a similar fate. In essence, Edom prescribed their own judgment. Joel wrote, "Edom shall be a desolate wilderness, for the violence against the children of Judah, because they have shed innocent blood in their land" (Joel 3:19). They had sown treachery, cruelty, and deceit and they would reap the same. (See Galatians 6:7.)

Babylon, possibly for Edom's treacherous services during the takeover of Judah, allowed some of the Edomites to settle in southern Palestine. Shortly afterward Nabateans, ancient people of Arabia, drove the rest of the Edomites out of Edom proper. Four centuries later the Maccabees completely subdued them and forced them to conform to Jewish laws and submit to the Jewish government prefects. Their territory became known as Idumaea. By the time of the siege of Jerusalem by Titus in AD 70, the Edomites had disappeared from the pages of history. Obadiah's prophecy had come true.

V. RESTORATION OF ISRAEL AND JUDAH AND EXTINCTION OF EDOM

Judah had sinned, but unlike Edom the people had sought and found a place of repentance. A remnant eventually returned from Babylon and repossessed the land that had been promised to their forefathers. However, the returning Jews found a land far different than the elders among them remembered.

This historical event fulfilled prophecy, but it also had a far-reaching spiritual application. When men and women return from the world of sin to a righteous relationship with Jesus Christ, it is far different from the lifestyle they remember. There has to be a spiritual erasure of those things such as Edom had treasured: pride, worldly wisdom and friends, and a false sense of indestructibility.

A. Edom Is Completely Eradicated

Extinction is a word we usually reserve for animal species like dinosaurs or wooly mammoths. But thinking of the extinction of an entire nation evokes a feeling of dismay.

> Tucked away in the southwestern corner of Colorado are the austere ruins of the Cliff Dwellers. Annually, thousands of tourists visit these remains of a once-thriving society and stand in respectful silence at the total loss of a people.

There is evidence Edom still existed as an independent nation in 586 BC, for Jeremiah mentioned that some of the Jews had moved to Edom (Jeremiah 40:11). In 587 BC Edom assisted Babylon by ransacking Jerusalem and turning fleeing captives over to them. Possibly as a reward for their services to Babylon during the war, Edom was allowed to relocate to Judean villages vacated after the captives were taken into Babylon. By 312 BC inscriptional evidence indicates the Nabateans had overrun the region of Edom. What a tragedy that Edom lost its land, bloodline, society, and existence when, as descendents of Isaac, they could have shared in the blessings of Jacob and received an everlasting inheritance.

No one can stand against the will and power of almighty God. A person could search through the history of the world and the entire Bible and not find one example where mankind, demons, or nations have triumphed over God's will.

B. Israel Is Restored and Revived

Obadiah prophesied of Judah's spiritual and national restoration. Mount Zion (verse 17) refers to Jerusalem, the city of David. Some day Mount Zion will be "holy" and restored to fullness of relationship with God. Not only will Israel be restored and revived spiritually, they will retake territories their enemies once occupied. The shining culmination of Israel's restoration will be when God ultimately rules over the world through His people. "The kingdom shall be the LORD'S" (Obadiah 21).

C. God Will Visit His People with Restoration and Revival

Isaiah spoke of a great re-gathering of the dispersed Jews. "And he shall set up an ensign for the nations, and shall assemble the outcasts of Israel, and gather together the dispersed of Judah from the four corners of the earth" (Isaiah 11:12). He wrote, "Behold, God is my salvation; I will trust, and not be afraid: for the LORD JEHOVAH is my strength and my song; he also is become my salvation. Therefore with joy shall ye draw water out of the wells of salvation" (Isaiah 12:2-3). "Ho, every one that thirsteth, come ye to the waters" (Isaiah 55:1).

On the last day of the Feast of Tabernacles, "Jesus stood and cried, saying, If any man thirst, let him come unto me, and drink. He that believeth on me, as the scripture hath said, out of his belly shall flow rivers of living water. (But this spake he of the Spirit, which they that believe on him should receive)" (John 7:37-39).

According to the *Nelson Study Bible*, during the Feast of Tabernacles a priest would take a golden pitcher from the Temple, fill it with water from the Pool of Siloam, and pour it on the altar as an offering to God. This was to remind the Jews of the relief and joy their forefathers felt when water gushed out of the rock during their travels through the parched wilderness. On the Day of Pentecost the Jews quenched their thirst with the water Jesus gives, "a well of water springing up into everlasting life" (John 4:14).

In the late nineteenth century and the early years of the twentieth century, dispersed Israelites began their journey back to the Land of Promise. Interestingly, this historical phenomenon took place in the same timeframe that the latter rain of the Holy Ghost began to fall, first in Topeka, Kansas, and then in Los Angeles in a humble building on Azusa Street. This triggered a great American revival of the Holy Ghost infilling that spread around the world.

The recognition in 1948 of Israel as a sovereign nation was a step toward the complete fulfillment of Obadiah's prophecy. We now look forward to the future kingdom of Jesus Christ as His people rule and reign with Him during the Millennium. The Holy Ghost continues to fall and God continues to restore Israel to her homeland. Surely the Lord will revisit Israel with great revival and "upon mount Zion . . . there shall be holiness" (Obadiah 17).

Internalizing the Message

The puff adder is a large, heavy-bodied African viper. When it feels threatened, the adder puffs itself out to look bigger than it really is. If it is touched in any way it strikes quickly.

Transparency 3

Transparency 3 says, "Prideful people are 'puffed up' and will not acknowledge a need to repent. They are destroyed by their own pride."

Paul said Christian love "is not puffed up" (I Corinthians 13:4). To the Colossians he wrote believers should not be beguiled by vain men who are "puffed up" by their fleshly minds. (See Colossians 2:18.) Prideful men try to look bigger than they really are. When their egos are threatened, they lash out. Pride distorts their thinking and causes them to make unwise decisions. Some people think of pride as the worst of all sins, because if a prideful person does not see his need to repent, he is often snared in his own trap. We as Christians should pray God will reveal any pride that lurks in our own minds or hearts. We cannot serve God with a pure heart until we do.

Edom's pride kept the nation from recognizing its need to repent. Unless a person repents, God eventually will reach the end of His longsuffering and will have no more mercy on that person. Noah preached righteousness to the wicked people of his day, warning them to repent or perish. The people did not repent, and consequently all the unbelievers perished. Jesus said, "Except ye repent, ye shall all likewise perish" (Luke 13:3). Yet, we should not look at repentance as a hard or grievous thing. The opportunity to repent is God's extending His mercy and forgiveness to anyone who comes to Him with a broken spirit and a contrite heart.

The Edomites chose their friends and allies unwisely, and when the day of trouble came, their allies turned against Edom. Whether or not we realize it, our friends influence our thinking patterns and behaviors. Therefore, it behooves us to choose our friends wisely. A loyal friend is one who "sticketh closer than a brother" (Proverbs 18:24). Solomon said, "A friend loveth at all times, and a brother is born for adversity" (Proverbs 17:17). Well-chosen friends will offer steadfast support and help in times of adversity.

Edom's leaders thought they were wise, but they led their nation down the wrong path and into destruction. We as the flock of God should follow the Good Shepherd wherever He leads. Thank God for leaders who, through the wisdom God gives, will guide us to everlasting life with Him.

REFLECTIONS

- God brought Edom down because of their pride. Discuss the effects of pride upon a person and why it leads to destruction.
- Nahum 1:2 says the Lord will take vengeance upon His adversaries. God said, "Vengeance is mine; I will repay" (Romans 12:19). Discuss.
- Discuss reasons why God was justified in annihilating Edom.
- Although both Edom and Israel had sinned, Obadiah prophesied the doom of Edom and the restoration of Israel. Discuss.
- Discuss what the church can do to advance the great end-time revival.

Jonah—Reluctant Obedience

5
week of 06.30.13

Lesson Text

Jonah 4:1-11

1 But it displeased Jonah exceedingly, and he was very angry.
2 And he prayed unto the LORD, and said, I pray thee, O LORD, was not this my saying, when I was yet in my country? Therefore I fled before unto Tarshish: for I knew that thou art a gracious God, and merciful, slow to anger, and of great kindness, and repentest thee of the evil.
3 Therefore now, O LORD, take, I beseech thee, my life from me; for it is better for me to die than to live.
4 Then said the LORD, Doest thou well to be angry?
5 So Jonah went out of the city, and sat on the east side of the city, and there made him a booth, and sat under it in the shadow, till he might see what would become of the city.
6 And the LORD God prepared a gourd, and made it to come up over Jonah, that it might be a shadow over his head, to deliver him from his grief. So Jonah was exceeding glad of the gourd.
7 But God prepared a worm when the morning rose the next day, and it smote the gourd that it withered.
8 And it came to pass, when the sun did arise, that God prepared a vehement east wind; and the sun beat upon the head of Jonah, that he fainted, and wished in himself to die, and said, It is better for me to die than to live.
9 And God said to Jonah, Doest thou well to be angry for the gourd? And he said, I do well to be angry, even unto death.
10 Then said the LORD, Thou hast had pity on the gourd, for the which thou hast not laboured, neither madest it grow; which came up in a night, and perished in a night.
11 And should not I spare Nineveh, that great city, wherein are more than sixscore thousand persons that cannot discern between their right hand and their left hand; and also much cattle?

Focus Thought

God's call reveals His heart, and our response to Him reveals our heart.

Focus Verses

Jonah 4:10-11

Then said the LORD, Thou hast had pity on the gourd, for the which thou hast not laboured, neither madest it grow; which came up in a night, and perished in a night: And should not I spare Nineveh, that great city, wherein are more than sixscore thousand persons that cannot discern between their right hand and their left hand; and also much cattle?

33

Learning to Obey God

by Richard M. Davis

From the American Kennel Club's website in an article titled "Getting Started in Obedience," training one's dog will accomplish the following achievements among other things:

• "Help correct nuisance behaviors such as jumping on people, digging, barking, and chewing, while providing mental and physical activities for your dog.

• "Deepen the bond between you and your dog, and to increase the enjoyment, companionship and satisfaction of your relationship with your dog.

• "Ensure your dog's safety and happiness" (*www.akc.org*, accessed March 20, 2012).

Wouldn't it be great if there were obedience training classes for people that would be effective in training us to obey God—the first time, every time, without fail or hesitation? It would save us so much pain and heartache. Unfortunately, it seems as if we humans always are slow to learn the lesson.

After the oft-repeated plight of the nations of Judah and Israel with regard to their relationship with God, one would think they would have learned that obedience to God is always the best policy. But it seemed as if they never learned. They fell into disobedience and idolatry time and again. Each time God sent judgment and chastised them, but only after much pain and sorrow did they once again turn to God and set their affections upon Him.

Jonah also learned the lesson of obedience the hard way—in the belly of the whale! It was a terrible way to learn obedience; but when he came out, he was ready to go to Nineveh. He went and preached to the people and they repented. It is amazing what happens when we obey God, and it surely saves us a lot of heartache.

Contemplating the Topic

The Book of Jonah is unique among the Minor Prophets. Instead of addressing Jonah's prophetic activity and messages to Israel, the book narrates the events surrounding God's call of Jonah to preach to the heathen city of Nineveh. Thus we will look at what God did and how Jonah reacted to discover the message of this book.

According to *The Old Testament Speaks*, Jonah's journey to Nineveh may have occurred sometime during the reign of Assurdan III of Assyria (773-756 BC). Many traumatizing events befell Assyria throughout these eighteen years: military losses, famine, domestic uprisings, and a plague. Then in 763 BC an eclipse of the sun terrified the city. The immensity and frequency of these tragedies may have prepared the Ninevites to receive the words of Jonah.

Jonah was aware of the suffering Aram had endured at the hands of the Assyrians. It is probable that Assyrian atrocities committed under the future King Tiglath-pileser III may have already been practiced during Jonah's time. Thus, from the human standpoint, Nineveh was the last place any Israelite prophet would choose as a target city for revival.

Some skeptics deem Jonah's deep sea experience a "whale of a tale." They also doubt Jonah's ability to communicate with the people of Nineveh, unless he somehow had learned Akaadian. Thus they treat Jonah's story as a myth, an allegory, or a parable. However, Jesus authenticated Jonah's experiences as historical fact when He pointed to the three days Jonah spent in the belly of the whale as a sign of His own three days in the tomb (Matthew 12:39-41).

Regardless of Jonah's initial rejection of the missionary call and his peevish response after he finally responded to the call, Jonah's presence and delivery had a powerful impact on the 120,000 people in Nineveh, and they repented.

Searching the Scriptures

I. THE DISOBEDIENCE OF THE PROPHET

A. Jonah's Missionary Call

Jonah was the son of the prophet Amittai of Gath-hepher, located in the territory of Zebulun (II Kings 14:25). His ministry occurred during the reign of Jeroboam II of Israel (c. 786-746). His call to Nineveh contained no details—just a directive to go there and cry against the city's wickedness, which had "come up" before the Lord. God did not tell him exactly what to say, and we are told only one line of his sermon: "Yet forty days, and Nineveh shall be overthrown" (Jonah 3:4).

Jonah did not understand why God would grant mercy to such wicked and violent people. He hated and feared the Assyrians. They would deride him and maybe kill him. Jonah decided to head in the opposite direction of Nineveh.

B. Jonah's Flight to Tarshish

The reluctant missionary purchased a ticket on a vessel bound for Tarshish on the southern coast of Spain, twenty-five hundred miles in the opposite direction from Nineveh. Jonah's desire to get away from God's call took him down: down to Joppa, down into the ship, down into the sides of the ship, down into the great fish's mouth, and down to the bottom of the sea.

Transparency   1

Transparency 1 shows a ship in a storm and says, "When we run from God's call, He will send storms, obstacles, and setbacks to get us to turn back to Him."

Jonah's disobedience reaped consequences for himself and others.

1. *Jonah fled from the presence of God.* His rebellious actions set in motion unexpected catastrophic results.

2. *Jonah's actions affected the lives of others.* A monster storm arose on the Mediterranean of the same magnitude as the Euroclydon that shipwrecked Paul on his voyage to Rome. According to the *Nelson Study Bible*, the descriptive word translated "tempestuous" in Acts 27:14 is the root of our word *typhoon*. The storm threatened the lives of everyone on board the ship.

3. *Distancing himself from God deepened Jonah's spiritual deadness.* Jonah was asleep when the shipmaster shook him awake. "All hands are on deck, but it's no use; we're going down. Call on your God to save us from death!" But Jonah did not pray; instead, he watched as the sailors cast lots, and the blame for the storm landed on him. They clamored for information about him, so he said, "I'm a Hebrew, and I fear the Lord, the Creator of all things."

They demanded, "Tell us what we should do so the sea will be calm."

Jonah still did not pray. But neither did he want his own folly to cause the deaths of the crew and passengers. So he said, "Cast me overboard, and the sea will grow calm."

The sailors tried to row to shore but made no headway. Finally they screamed into the storm, entreating Jonah's God for help.

C. Jonah Thrown Overboard and Swallowed by a Great Fish

Skeptics doubt a fish could swallow a man whole; and they are sure a man could not survive three days in a fish's belly. On the other hand, believers know (1) God prepared a great fish; and (2) God can work miracles. However, even believers may wonder why God used this particular method to rescue Jonah from his own disobedience. We can find some obvious reasons in Scripture.

Jonah thought his three-day confinement in the fish's roiling belly was like being in Hell (2:2). This near-death experience impressed upon Jonah a sense of the judgment disobedience brings. Further, if he did not warn the people of Nineveh, judgment and doom would destroy them and God would hold Jonah personally responsible.

Jonah's deliverance taught him that God extends the same grace, mercy, and kindness to the heathen that He bestows upon His chosen people. God loves all souls and will go to any length in order to deliver just one from destruction.

Jonah's deliverance from the belly of the fish typifies Jesus Christ's resurrection from the grave (Matthew 12:39-40). The same resurrection power can deliver every living soul who will repent.

II. THE DELIVERANCE OF THE PROPHET

A. Jonah's Prayer

Ever since the inception of the Hebrew race they had been a stiff-necked people. (See Deuteronomy 31:27.) A stiff-necked person will not turn his head. Jonah ran from God without turning around or looking back. But his "fishy" ordeal took the kinks out of his neck, and he turned to look again toward the Lord's holy Temple (Jonah 2:4). At last he uttered desperate prayers and promised to keep his vows. He acknowledged "salvation is of the LORD" (2:9). Jonah's repentance was more than empty words. He turned from his rebellion to do God's will.

First, Jonah changed his mind and heart. Before he repented, he had harbored a deep-seated dislike for a people he saw as the enemy. Perhaps he had a premonition Assyria would destroy the northern kingdom of Israel forty years down the road, and it hindered him from preaching a message of deliverance to Israel's nemesis. However, repentance requires a change of heart. Jonah's repentance caused him to turn to his enemies and preach a message of deliverance.

Second, Jonah changed his direction. At the time of his first missionary call, Jonah had deliberately run in the opposite direction of God and His will. His story makes it clear that rebellion and disobedience will always end up in the belly of Hell. From the midst of torment and corruption, Jonah cried out in repentance and vowed to change his direction and his ways.

B. God's Answer

Jonah's disobedience dropped him straight into the belly of Hell. The paths of many who run from God lead to unexpected, frightening places where the monsters of affliction swallow them whole. Broken homes, financial loss, addiction, depression, loneliness, and a myriad of other tragedies befall the rebellious. However, in these dark hours those who turn to God in repentance can be released from their torment, and turn to do God's will.

Jonah's experience teaches us that although we repent and receive the grace of God, we will still pay the price for willful rebellion. How we respond to the Lord's discipline determines the

benefit derived from that discipline. When a child responds to discipline with more rebellion and more willful disobedience he is only inviting additional discipline. However, if he responds with brokenness and receives the discipline with a changed attitude, then he will be able to receive instruction that promotes wholesome, godly character.

III. THE DECLARATION OF GOD'S MESSAGE THROUGH THE PROPHET

Presumably, the whale vomited Jonah upon the coast of northern Palestine, the closest starting point from which to make the journey of over four hundred miles to Nineveh. No sooner had Jonah landed on the beach than God said, "Arise, go unto Nineveh, that great city, and preach unto it the preaching that I bid thee" (3:2).

Transparency / 2

Transparency 2 says that Nineveh was God's target city for revival and quotes a portion of Romans 9:15.

A. The Threat of Judgment

Jonah's second call from God provides strong evidence that God deals with His servants again after they have repented and have been forgiven of their mistakes. Unlike human nature, God does not hold grudges. He forgives and is willing to give us a second chance.

Further, God often uses the circumstances in the life of the messenger to relate to the condition of those to whom he is sent. God gave Jonah a second chance after granting Him forgiveness and grace; now Jonah served as a living object lesson that though the Ninevites had committed a multitude of sins, God was willing to save them if they would repent.

That God intended to grant mercy to Nineveh can be seen in two powerful ways. First, God sent a preacher. Nineveh deserved total destruction; yet, Jonah's message did not address their specific sins. Apparently the vileness of their sins made them conscious of their own condition, for the king proclaimed a fast and a time of mourning. "Let man and beast be covered with sackcloth, and cry mightily unto God; yea, let them turn every one from his evil way, and from the violence that is in their hands" (3:8). God sends a preacher to those He intends to save.

The second declaration of God's merciful intention is He gives the condemned a space to repent. In Noah's day, God gave the wicked time to repent while Noah was building the ark. Even after Noah entered the ark, God waited seven days before He closed the door and rained down judgment on a wicked generation. For Nineveh, He set aside a forty-day grace period to give the inhabitants the opportunity to respond to Jonah's message. God gives everyone a period of time to respond to His call to repentance, but that period will have a definite end.

B. The City-Wide Repentance

To the Ninevites, Jonah appeared as one who narrowly had escaped the ghastly jaws of death. His skin had bleached in the fish's belly; his sunken eyes still reflected the horror; his gravelly voice pierced their hearts like a sword as he proclaimed, "Yet forty days, and Nineveh shall be overthrown" (3:4).

Jonah's message affected the entire city of Nineveh, from the king to the lowliest pauper—even the children and animals. The people believed God, proclaimed a fast, and put on sackcloth. Genuine repentance leaves nothing unaffected. There is no person too young or too old. No individual is too lofty or too lowly to be exempt from responding to the message from God.

God is concerned about every area of our lives. Nothing is too great or too insignificant to merit His attention. The Book of Jonah reminds us we must turn from every wicked way, surrender to the lordship of Jesus Christ, and do the will of God.

> *God is concerned about every area of our lives.*

C. The Judgment Averted

Total surrender to God results in averting the judgment of God. Jonah turned from his wrong direction and his wrong thinking. Nineveh turned from its evil and wicked ways. Then God turned from the intended judgment and granted mercy to Nineveh. Repentance is the acting of turning. And once the repentant one turns from condemnation, he faces mercy.

IV. THE DISPLEASURE OF THE PROPHET

A. Jonah's Heart Revealed

Even though Jonah knew he had lost the battle of the wills, he still waged his own personal war.

1. *Jonah's Petulant Prayer (Jonah 4:1-3).* Jonah's reaction to God's mercy on Nineveh reveals a nature steered by uncontrolled emotions. Jonah was angry! Possibly his vehement preaching served as a vent for his wrath against a country that had abused many other nations and was a threat to Jonah's own countrymen. He felt the evil city deserved the judgment God had planned. Jonah accused God, "I ran from Nineveh because I knew You would not rain down fire and brimstone; if they repented, You would change Your mind and rain down mercy." Jonah knew—as well as all Israelites knew—about the mercy of God.

> "The LORD is merciful and gracious, slow to anger, and plenteous in mercy. He will not always chide: neither will he keep his anger for ever" (Psalm 103:8-9). (See also Exodus 34:6-7; Nehemiah 9:17; Psalm 86:15; Joel 2:13.)

But Jonah had erred by thinking God manifested mercy, forbearance, and grace only when dealing with His own people, not with the world in general. The possibility Nineveh might be spared upset Jonah so much he wished to die.

2. *God's Searching Question (Jonah 4:4).* God asked Jonah, "What right do you have to be angry?" After all, God had mercifully kept Jonah alive in the belly of the fish when he should have let him die. When Jonah repented, God caused the fish to swim to the coast of Palestine and deposit the reluctant missionary on the shore. God had blessed Jonah with the same mercy He now was granting to the Ninevites. Jonah had no right to be angry at God for extending mercy to heathens.

This idea was so foreign to first-century Jews that it took Peter and some believing Jews time to grasp the reach of God's grace. They thought God's New Covenant grace had been sent to them exclusively. God went to great lengths to get Peter to "unlearn" this concept. He sent a vision of a sheet being lowered from Heaven, full of beasts, creeping things, and fowls. A voice said, "Rise, Peter; kill, and eat" (Acts 10:13). Like any observant Jew, Peter refused. This happened three times, and then Peter was summoned to the door. There he met a delegation from Cornelius, asking Peter to come to Caesarea and preach Christ. Peter did, and while he was yet preaching the Holy Ghost fell on Cornelius's family. The Jews who had accompanied Peter "were astonished, . . . because that on the Gentiles also was poured out the gift of the Holy Ghost. For they heard them speak with tongues, and magnify God" (Acts 10:45-46). God offers mercy and salvation to everyone.

3. *Jonah Sulking outside the City (Jonah 4:5)*. Paul said, "Where sin abounded, grace did much more abound" (Romans 5:20). The Book of Jonah reveals the great grace of God toward the "great city" of Nineveh that needed to hear a message of repentance. God had left nothing to chance; He prepared a man, a storm, and a fish.

Jonah chapter 4 narrows our view from the mission back to the man. He survived the whale, but would he survive the worm God prepared?

B. God's Heart Revealed

When people fail through disobedience, they often feel as though there is no second change to repair their relationship with God. Jonah's story reveals God's heart through the great grace He gives to the undeserving. But it is not enough simply to serve God mechanically. God wants us to serve wholeheartedly: "Not with eyeservice, as men-pleasers; but as the servants of Christ, doing the will of God from the heart" (Ephesians 6:6).

V. THE DEMONSTRATION OF THE SOVEREIGN MERCY OF GOD

A. The Plant

While the city of Nineveh mourned, Jonah climbed a hill to find a good spot to see what would happen. He built a small shelter and sat in its shadow. Then he noticed a plant pushing vigorously out of the ground. It grew beside the shelter and cast enough shade to shelter the prophet's head. "Exceeding glad," he enjoyed the shade all day while the city mourned. Nothing happened.

B. The Pity

Transparency 3

Transparency 3 asks, "Jonah survived the whale, but would he survive the worm?"

The next day Jonah noticed a large worm gorging itself on the leaves of his plant. Soon the stalk withered and died. Then a hot, dry wind buffeted him, and the sun beat on him without mercy.

It is one thing to pity someone else. Pitying someone else means to have compassion on the person. It is being like God. "Like as a father pitieth his children, so the LORD pitieth them that fear him" (Psalm 103:13).

It is another thing, however, to pity oneself. Self-pity arises out of the heart of a self-centered person. He craves the sympathy, support, and encouragement of others, thinking it will make him feel better. He walks around with a martyr's complex. His misery makes everyone around him miserable. Soon he begins to grate on them like sandpaper.

> *Self-pity arises out of the heart of a self-centered person.*

Jonah had climbed the hill to see the hoped-for destruction of the lost city, but he got sidetracked by his own misery. Like a true martyr he cried, "It is better for me to die than to live." (See Jonah 4:8.) God asked, "What right have you to be angry that the gourd died?" Jonah pouted, "I have a right to be angry, even unto death."

Exasperated, God said, "Here you are, pitying yourself for the loss of a gourd while thousands of lost people are trying to find their way back to Me. I pity them and so should you."

Internalizing the Message

Jonah's misconceptions and his self-centeredness caused him to run from the call of God. We should strive to understand the heart of God. He is not willing that any should perish. He wants all to come to repentance. His gospel, His mercy, and His love extend to all people, not just a select few. While we crave His attention, we should not begrudge someone else receiving what we have received, whether or not we think they deserve it. After all, what makes us think we deserve anything good from God? We ourselves have made mistakes and needed God's forgiveness. There is room at the foot of the Cross for all people. If we are to be like God, we will have compassion and mercy on others who need Him and do what we can to see them saved.

God held Jonah responsible; he was the man for the mission; God loved Jonah too much to let him go. In reality, we cannot escape the call of God. Even if we never fulfill it, we will never forget the call. God will let nothing and no one fall from His grasp. The only way we can escape from His call is to run away. But God loves us too much to let us go without a fight and prepares obstacles, storms, and setbacks, trying to get us to turn around. Hosea described it as hedging "up the way with thorns" (Hosea 2:6).

Jonah repented, and God gave him a second chance to participate in the mission. Even when we fail miserably, if we repent God will forgive and offer us a second chance. He has not changed His mind: we are still the person for the mission. We know we are not capable of completing the mission, but if He has called us, He will give us the wisdom, power, and ability to perform it.

Jonah, instead of exulting in the Lord for the phenomenal success of his preaching, climbed a hill to watch what would happen. He did not pity the wicked sinners of Nineveh. He wanted them to burn. When God gives us victories, we should rejoice over the sinners who repent and give glory to Him instead of secretly hoping they will get what they deserve. After all, God did not give us what we deserved. "He hath not dealt with us after our sins; nor rewarded us according to our iniquities" (Psalm 103:10). Instead, the Lord "laid on him [Jesus Christ] the iniquity of us all" (Isaiah 53:6). He would rather forgive than punish, and in order to remove our punishment, He bore it Himself on the Cross.

REFLECTIONS

- Jonah could not understand why God would show mercy to Nineveh. Peter and the rest of the Jews could not understand why God poured out the Holy Ghost on the Gentiles. Place this in today's context and discuss.
- Most people have no problem with God's sovereign rule in nature. But when the sovereign will of God comes into opposition with our contrary human will, a problem develops. Discuss.
- Jonah was self-centered. Discuss possible outcomes when God uses self-centered people to do His will. Suggest ways for self-centered people to think less of themselves and more of God and others.
- Jonah's initial disobedience and subsequent obedience affected other people. Discuss how others are affected by our own actions, whether negative or positive.
- Discuss the true meaning of repentance.
- Discuss reasons why God prepared the plant, the worm, and the east wind. What was He trying to teach Jonah?

6
week of
07.07.13

Micah—A Remnant Gathered, Restored, and Forgiven

Lesson Text

Micah 7:11-20

11 In the day that thy walls are to be built, in that day shall the decree be far removed.

12 In that day also he shall come even to thee from Assyria, and from the fortified cities, and from the fortress even to the river, and from sea to sea, and from mountain to mountain.

13 Notwithstanding the land shall be desolate because of them that dwell therein, for the fruit of their doings.

14 Feed thy people with thy rod, the flock of thine heritage, which dwell solitarily in the wood, in the midst of Carmel: let them feed in Bashan and Gilead, as in the days of old.

15 According to the days of thy coming out of the land of Egypt will I shew unto him marvellous things.

16 The nations shall see and be confounded at all their might: they shall lay their hand upon their mouth, their ears shall be deaf.

17 They shall lick the dust like a serpent, they shall move out of their holes like worms of the earth: they shall be afraid of the LORD our God, and shall fear because of thee.

18 Who is a God like unto thee, that pardoneth iniquity, and passeth by the transgression of the remnant of his heritage? he retaineth not his anger for ever, because he delighteth in mercy.

19 He will turn again, he will have compassion upon us; he will subdue our iniquities; and thou wilt cast all their sins into the depths of the sea.

20 Thou wilt perform the truth to Jacob, and the mercy to Abraham, which thou hast sworn unto our fathers from the days of old.

Focus Thought

We never wander so far from God that we cannot be brought back and forgiven by Him.

Focus Verse

Micah 7:18

Who is a God like unto thee, that pardoneth iniquity, and passeth by the transgression of the remnant of his heritage? He retaineth not his anger for ever, because he delighteth in mercy.

The Hope of Restoration and Forgiveness
by Richard M. Davis

America has quite a love affair with its automobiles. Cars in this nation are not just a means of transportation from home to work and to run errands. Cars take on a special significance to the individuals who drive them and represent a measure of affections, emotions, and personalities. Consequently, the restoration of classic cars in America has become a booming, cottage industry for thousands of individuals.

I must confess I also took up this special interest in classic cars when I purchased a restored 1956 Nash Metropolitan. Since that time I have been awakened to how big this industry really is—through periodicals, car shows, and specialized parts suppliers. One thing I have observed among the classic car aficionados is amazing: some individuals never see a rusting heap in a junkyard as worthless and irreparable. Rather, they see potential; they see a future project. They see—through much time, work, and commitment—what a timeless classic automobile could come out of the abandoned, rusting shell of what once was a fine mode of transportation.

The prophet Micah never saw an automobile and he belonged to no classic car clubs, but he saw the same commitment to restoration that car enthusiasts today possess. What he saw, however, was God's commitment to the restoration of His people. No matter how hopeless the picture of Israel's and Judah's states seemed to be at times, God never gave up on His people. He continued to send the message of hope for restoration and forgiveness to them. "If my people. . . ." If they would repent, He would forgive and restore.

No person is a hopeless case; no sinner is too far from God. No individual is a lost cause. If we will repent of our sins, turning to God for redemption, He will forgive us and restore us.

I. A REMNANT GATHERED
  A. Prediction of Wrath against Israel and Judah
  B. The Doom of the Wealthy Oppressors
II. A REMNANT RESTORED
  A. The Promise of Restoration
  B. Denunciation of Rulers, False Prophets, and Priests
  C. The Glory of the Millennial Reign
  D. The Promise of the Messiah's Coming
  E. Israel on Trial
  F. The Sad State of the Nation
III. A REMNANT FORGIVEN
  A. Future Blessings for Israel
  B. God's Powerful Forgiveness

Contemplating the Topic

To the casual observer, Micah might appear to be a very "minor" prophet—one of little significance. He was not as silver tongued as his contemporary, the aristocratic Isaiah who was the confidant of kings and statesmen. Compared to Isaiah's eloquent literary style, Micah's was "rough and rugged." He was probably a peasant farmer or a craftsman possibly looked down upon by the city folk of Jerusalem. His own generation did not readily receive him, and modern-day scholars have not given him as much academic attention as other Old Testament prophets such as Isaiah, Daniel, and Hosea.

However, Micah is arguably the most quoted prophet who ever lived. In between his indictments and warnings of impending doom, Micah offered powerful words of hope that world leaders and common people alike have clung to throughout the centuries. He gave three notable promises.

1. "They shall beat their swords into plowshares, and their spears into pruninghooks: nation shall not lift up a sword against nation, neither shall they learn war any more" (Micah 4:3).

In 1959, the Russian government presented a monument to the United Nations inscribed with Micah 4:3. It is ironic that Micah's words of hope should be placed at this prominent international crossroads in New York City by a nation whose leaders and philosophers were atheists.

Famous songwriters have borrowed this theme, including Michael Jackson in his song "Heal the World": "In my heart I feel you are all my brothers, create a world with no fear; together we'll . . . see the nations turn their swords into plowshares (*www.azlyrics.com/lyrics/michaeljackson/healtheworld.html*).

Micah's message has been quoted in the speeches of US presidents and recited at inaugural ceremonies. It shines as a glimmer of hope penetrating the darkness of a world reeling in military conflict.

2. "But thou, Beth-lehem Ephratah, though thou be little among the thousands of Judah, yet out of thee shall he come forth unto me that is to be ruler in Israel; whose goings forth have been from of old, from everlasting" (Micah 5:2).

The inquiry of the three wise men from the East about a newborn king of the Jews infuriated Herod the Great whose Idumean blood disqualified him from sitting on the throne of David. (See II Samuel 7.) Nevertheless, he had procured the governorship of Galilee when his father, Antipater, persuaded the Roman Senate to appoint him. With assassination in mind, Herod sent for the priests and scribes and inquired craftily where this newborn king could be found. Citing Micah's prophecy they answered "Bethlehem." (See Matthew 2:5-6.) Jesus, the newborn king, was the "root and the offspring of David" (Revelation 22:16). (See also Isaiah 11:1.) As the offspring of David, He was the "Branch"; as the root of David, He was God.

3. "He hath shewed thee, O man, what is good; and what doth the LORD require of thee, but to do justly, and to love mercy, and to walk humbly with thy God?" (Micah 6:8).

Here Micah, the rough and rugged writer, encapsulated eloquently the essence of the Hebrew faith. His intent was not to attack the Jews' sacrificial system but their belief they could please God merely through external religious acts. Micah challenged this misconception with the truth—even extreme sacrifice did not please God if it did not stem from inward righteousness and a right relationship with God. (See Micah 6:6-8.)

The last twelve books in the Old Testament are called "minor" because of the brevity of the prophets' messages. But as we have seen, Micah's book is far from minor in its far-reaching significance.

Searching the Scriptures

Micah's forty-year ministry spanned the reigns of three Judean kings: Jotham (from c. 740 BC), Ahaz, and Hezekiah (until c. 699 BC). During this time Israel consisted of two separate countries: Israel in the north and Judah in the south. Micah prophesied to both Samaria and Jerusalem, the capital cities of the northern and southern kingdoms respectively.

I. A REMNANT GATHERED

Transparency 1

Transparency 1 quotes a portion of Micah 2:12.

The Book of Micah consists of three major divisions, each beginning with an oracle of doom and ending with an oracle of hope. The beginning of each division is marked with the imperative "Hear" (1:2; 3:1; 6:1).

A. Prediction of Wrath against Israel and Judah

Without preamble Micah launched a fierce indictment against Samaria and Jerusalem. "I will make Samaria a heap of ruins in the field. . . . All her carved images shall be beaten to pieces . . . all her idols I will lay desolate" (Micah 1:6-7, NKJV). The contagion of Samaria's obsession for the cultic worship of Baal had been caught by Jerusalem, which sacrificed to idols in high places and even brought idols into the Temple. The incurable wounds of Samaria had "come unto Judah . . . even to Jerusalem" (Micah 1:9).

Micah lived to see the ruin of Samaria. According to *Unger's Bible Dictionary*, Assyria invaded the northern kingdom in 722 BC, led away two hundred thousand captives, put an end to Samaria's independence, and brought in heathen colonists. Micah did not live to experience the ruin of the southern kingdom, but predicted evil would come down "from the LORD unto the gate of Jerusalem" (Micah 1:12). Judah's downfall happened in two major deportations, the first in 606 BC when Babylon carried off the nobility of Judah, and again in 587 BC when Babylon took into captivity all but the poorest of the land.

B. The Doom of the Wealthy Oppressors

In Micah 2 he decried the social evils of the day. He condemned the greedy nobles, unethical merchants, murderers, and the people's dysfunctional family relationships. He advocated for the downtrodden and condemned those who plotted to steal from the poor.

Micah then accused false prophets who told people only what they wanted to hear. In contrast, Micah's desire to please God drove him to deal only with truth. He refused to be a people pleaser.

II. A REMNANT RESTORED

In every dispensation there has been a plan of salvation for that time, a preacher to declare truth, deliverance for the godly, and judgment for the wicked. God has redeemed a remnant in every Bible dispensation.

Transparency 2

Transparency 2 states, "God has redeemed a remnant in every dispensation."

A. The Promise of Restoration

Micah's prophecy of restoration has dual reference. It refers not only to Micah's generation but also to the future Jewish remnant that will turn to Christ and be saved in the end times. (See Micah 2:12-13.) The word *remnant* signifies a group of people who do not merit judgment because they have been faithful to the Word of the Lord.

God's judgment always leaves room for mercy if people will humble themselves and repent. Today's revival efforts are often thought of in terms of advertising and finance, and finding an evangelist who will draw a big crowd. The biblical formula for revival is quite different, however.

"If my people, which are called by my name, shall humble themselves, and pray, and seek my face, and turn from their wicked ways; then will I hear from heaven, and will forgive their sin, and will heal their land" (II Chronicles 7:14).

Humility, prayer, and obedience are God's prerequisites to revival. True revival cannot be produced any other way.

B. Denunciation of Rulers, False Prophets, and Priests

In the third chapter, Micah prophesied of the destruction of Jerusalem as the consequence of the iniquity of evil rulers, false prophets, and priests. Rulers expected a monetary reward for making judicial pronouncements; priests expected a fee for instructing the people; false prophets expected money for their divinations and flattery of the people's every whim.

The tragedy of a nation's drift away from God and morality begins with its leaders. Every dark period in the history of the world has begun with wickedness in high places.

Corrupt immoral leaders bring about the destruction of their people and country. Oh, for national leaders who will humble themselves and seek the face of God. Oh, for spiritual leaders who will not bend to the pressures of the times but will speak the truth in love.

Even in times when godlessness prevails, God will always send a prophet or preacher to guide people in the way of deliverance—and there is always a remnant who will follow that prophet. These men and women of God pay the price of the displeasure, resentment, and sometimes hatred shown by people who, according to Paul's quaint expression, have itching ears. (See II Timothy 4:3.) Declaring truth in the face of hate, rampant idolatry, wickedness, and violence requires courage and boldness which, like Micah's, comes only from God.

"But truly I am full of power by the spirit of the LORD, and of judgment, and of might, to declare unto Jacob his transgression, and to Israel his sin" (Micah 3:8).

In the early 1900s God led Andrew Urshan to Leningrad, Russia, where he found more than 150 people hungry for Jesus Name baptism. He waded into the icy river and stayed "for over two hours baptizing the anxious converts. The power of God would fall upon them in the water, and for a long time they would be shaking under the power, praising God, and receiving the Baptism of the Holy Spirit" (The Life of Andrew Bar David Urshan, Stockton, CA.: Apostolic Press, 1967). Brother Urshan felt God had led these people to "be baptized into His Name . . . so that they might be saved from the terrible Bolshevik massacres which followed a year later." At least one thousand baptized believers survived the holocaust.

After the revolution Vladimir Lenin and his successors labeled Christians as outcasts and placed a ban on Bibles. For seventy-four years, until the end of the Cold War, Christians were denied jobs and education and imprisoned, tortured, and killed. Yet truth prevailed through the power of the Holy Ghost in these believers, and an underground revival began to spread to many parts of Russia.

C. The Glory of the Millennial Reign

Throughout history mankind has tried to institute world peace by means of antiproliferation treaties, political unions, and peace pacts by the score. For instance, the League of Nations formed after World War I and the United Nations formed after World War II represent mankind's attempts to solve the world's problems. Yet we continue to wage wars.

The fulfillment of the prophecies of Micah covers a vast amount of time and history. Some have already been fulfilled, but the prophecies of chapter 4 project into the future. They give great hope of a time on earth when God's peace shall reign.

> *"And many nations shall come, and say, Come, and let us go up to the mountain of the LORD, and to the house of the God of Jacob; and he will teach us of his ways, and we will walk in his paths: for the law shall go forth of Zion, and the word of the LORD from Jerusalem" (Micah 4:2).*

Just before the Millennium the Lord will call to Himself a remnant of His dispersed flock and bring them to the Holy Land, where they finally will fulfill God's desire that they be a holy nation, a kingdom of priests (Exodus 19:5-6). Jesus Christ will set up His earthly kingdom in Jerusalem and all nations will come to worship Him and bring gifts to the Temple. The gates of the Holy City will be open continually (Isaiah 60:11).

Rulers of nations cannot solve the world's problems. Only a righteous and just God can heal the nations and bring world peace. Thus Micah's message has become the hope of peace for all mankind.

D. The Promise of the Messiah's Coming

Micah 5:2-3 contains the greatest promise of the ages.

> *"But thou, Beth-lehem Ephratah, though thou be little among the thousands of Judah, yet out of thee shall he come forth unto me that is to be ruler in Israel; whose goings forth have been from of old, from everlasting. Therefore will he give them up, until the time that she which travaileth hath brought forth" (Micah 5:2-3).*

In this prophecy Micah saw not only the birth of the Messiah, but also the time when Jesus Christ will rule and reign in the Millennium. Notice the detail of this prophecy. Micah named a specific birthplace for the Messiah, "Beth-lehem Ephratah," which locates the village in a known region in Judah. The fulfillment of this prophecy arrived with the birth of the Messiah when Jesus Christ was born of a virgin maiden in the obscure village of Bethlehem. (See Luke 2; Matthew 1:18-25.) Although Jesus' mother was a peasant, royal blood flowed through His veins because of her lineage through Nathan, the son of King David. (See Luke 3:31.) Jesus truly was born "King of the Jews" (Matthew 2:2). His birth was like no other, because He is "from everlasting" (Micah 5:2).

The second component of this prophecy still awaits fulfillment when Jesus Christ, the eternal "God with us" (Matthew 1:23) will reign in Jerusalem. Jesus' divinity guarantees the eternality of His reign. Isaiah foretold, "Of the increase of his government and peace there shall be no end" (Isaiah 9:7).

E. Israel on Trial

"Hear now what the LORD says: Arise, plead your case" (Micah 6:1, NKJV). Micah's summons to the Lord's court of law seemed to echo throughout Israel.

> *"Hear ye, O mountains, the LORD's controversy, and ye strong foundations of the earth: for the LORD hath a controversy with his people, and he will plead with Israel" (Micah 6:2).*

The prophet opened the case with a brief review of Israel's history: their miraculous deliverance from slavery in Egypt through the leadership of Moses, Aaron, and Miriam; their blessing on the plains of Moab when the king of Moab hired Balaam to curse God's people but out of his mouth came abundant blessings; their miracle crossing of the River Jordan from Shittim, their last encampment before crossing the Jordan, to Gilgal, their first encampment upon entering the Promised Land.

The antidote for depression and discouragement is to look back to the miracles God has provided. Rehearsing God's blessings erects a protective seawall when the waves of hurt and disappointment rush in. "Call to remembrance the former days. . . . Cast not away therefore your confidence" (Hebrews 10:32, 35). The miracles of the past give faith for the future.

Like a zealous prosecutor, Micah seated Israel in the witness box and began a series of leading questions that summarized his case: "Wherewith shall I come before the LORD, and bow myself before the high God? shall I come before him with burnt offerings, with calves of a year old? Will the LORD be pleased with thousands of rams, or with ten thousands of rivers of oil? shall I give my firstborn for my transgression, the fruit of my body for the sin of my soul?" (Micah 6:6-7).

In verse 8, Micah then declared the critical point of his case, three requirements that apply to all believers, not just the Jews.

> "He hath shewed thee, O man, what is good; and what doth the LORD require of thee . . ."

• "to do justly . . ." God requires honesty in our relationships and deeds, not only with our fellow man but with Him. We can fool those around us, but we never can fool God, for He knows us better than we know ourselves. We should rid ourselves of all pretense and dissimulation before coming to Him. He can read the thoughts and intents of the heart.

• "to love mercy . . ." God always balances His judgment with mercy, and we must do the same. During the times in life when we must make judgment calls, it is important to choose carefully between good and evil. Further, there is a difference in attitude between judging rightly and being judgmental. God asks us not only to judge rightly, but to do it through eyes and hearts full of mercy.

• "to walk humbly with thy God." Once again we are reminded that spiritual success is connected to humility. Arrogance is always the wrong approach to God. Realizing how incompetent we are in comparison to His awesome power gives us no alternative but to approach Him with humility. James wrote, "Humble yourselves in the sight of the Lord, and he shall lift you up" (James 4:10).

F. The Sad State of the Nation

Anguish poured from the prophet's heart: "Woe is me. . . . The good man is perished out of the earth: and there is none upright among men" (Micah 7:1-2). Micah mourned because of the wickedness in Israel. There was wholehearted ungodliness, chaos, and bloodshed. Every individual was intent on destroying his brother. Governors and judges continually schemed to do evil and pervert justice.

After delivering a seven-verse indictment of Israel's sins, Micah pointed to the only remedy.

> "Therefore I will look unto the LORD; I will wait for the God of my salvation: my God will hear me. Rejoice not against me, O mine enemy: when I fall, I shall arise; when I sit in darkness, the LORD shall be a light unto me" (Micah 7:7-8).

The world offers elusive, uncertain hope: "I hope things will get better. I hope I can make it." But great and tangible hope can be found in God's Word! "Which hope we have as an anchor of the soul, both sure and stedfast" (Hebrews 6:19). This sure and steadfast hope spurs us to get back up when we fall, which is the key to spiritual success. No matter how many times a person may slip up, success will come if he keeps getting up. The only people God cannot use are those who give up and lie in defeat.

III. A REMNANT FORGIVEN

The word *remnant* appears six times in the Book of Micah. In today's language, a remnant means a leftover, like the piece of cloth that remains on the end of a large bolt after the rest of the material has been sold at the full price. Generally, what is left on a bolt is marked down and sold for much less.

Transparency 3

Transparency 3 says, "In the biblical context, a remnant refers to a chosen group of people who have repented, turned to God, and found forgiveness."

However, the biblical reference to a remnant has quite a different connotation. In a biblical context a *remnant* refers to a chosen group of people who have been called out of darkness into light. They are those who have repented, turned to God, and found forgiveness.

A. Future Blessings for Israel

Once again Micah's prophecies have dual reference. At the same time he interceded for the people of his generation, he also pointed to a future time when a remnant of Israel will return to God and receive His blessings.

He recalled the promise God gave to Abraham that from his seed would come a Savior who would bring truth and mercy to the world.

> "Thou wilt perform the truth to Jacob, and the mercy to Abraham,

which thou hast sworn unto our fathers from the days of old" (Micah 7:20).

The steadfast faithfulness of God guaranteed the fulfillment of His promises to the patriarchs. "My lovingkindness will I not utterly take from him, nor suffer my faithfulness to fail" (Psalm 89:33). The birth, life, ministry, and death of Jesus Christ fulfilled the Lord's promise to Abraham that through him "all the families of the earth [would] be blessed" (Genesis 12:3).

B. God's Powerful Forgiveness

Micah prophesied of a time when Israel will return to God and find forgiveness.

"Who is a God like unto thee, that pardoneth iniquity, and passeth by the transgression of the remnant of his heritage? he retaineth not his anger for ever, because he delighteth in mercy. He will turn again, he will have compassion upon us; he will subdue our iniquities; and thou wilt cast all their sins into the depths of the sea" (Micah 7:18-19).

What a comfort to know God will not retain His wrath forever! He pardons iniquity and forgives transgressions. Isaiah expressed this eloquently.

"I [the LORD] dwell in the high and holy place, with him also that is of a contrite and humble spirit. . . . I have seen his [wicked] ways, and will heal him: I will lead him also, and restore comforts unto him and to his mourners" (Isaiah 57:15, 18).

Internalizing the Message

The Old Testament prophets dealt primarily with the Jews; however, it would be interesting to know what warnings they would thunder to the church today. In the New Testament at the end of the first century, the apostle John, like Micah, wrote to believers to urge, "He that hath an ear, let him hear what the Spirit saith unto the churches" (Revelation 3:22).

Have we like the church of Laodicea grown lukewarm, materialistic, and self-reliant? John counseled Laodicea to buy gold, white raiment, and eye salve from God. Our relationship with God can be restored once we have been tried in the fire, have been clothed in the garment of His righteousness, and have had our eyesight restored.

To the church of Philadelphia, John wrote, "Because thou hast kept the word of my patience, I also will keep thee from the hour of temptation. . . . Behold, I come quickly: hold that fast which thou hast, that no man take thy crown" (Revelation 3:10-11). Faithful believers will inherit a new name and a place in the New Jerusalem in the presence of God. (See Revelation 3:12.)

The church of today stands at a strategic place—the threshold of the fulfillment of many prophecies. God calls for His church to be spiritually alert by heeding the words of the apostles, prophets, evangelists, pastors, and teachers who observe the signs of the times. Jesus said, "When these things begin to come to pass, then look up, and lift up your heads; for your redemption draweth nigh" (Luke 21:28).

REFLECTIONS

- Micah was "minor"; Isaiah was "major." Did their messages carry equal weight? Reflect on the wide range of preaching styles and personalities of men and women God uses today. Read Micah 3:8 and discuss.
- Discuss the biblical meaning of the word *remnant* and the significance it holds for God's people in any age of time.
- Discuss the true keys to revival as given in II Chronicles 7:14.
- The twenty-first-century church stands in a strategic place in the kingdom era. Prophecies are being fulfilled before our eyes. Discuss the importance of staying spiritually alert and heeding the messages we hear from the Word of God.
- Discuss the contrast between the hope the world offers and the hope God offers. How should a true and living hope affect us in times of discouragement?

Nahum— God Hates Sin

7
week of 07.14.13

Lesson Text

Nahum 1:1-9, 12-15

1 The burden of Nineveh. The book of the vision of Nahum the Elkoshite.

2 God is jealous, and the LORD revengeth; the LORD revengeth, and is furious; the LORD will take vengeance on his adversaries, and he reserveth wrath for his enemies.

3 The LORD is slow to anger, and great in power, and will not at all acquit the wicked: the LORD hath his way in the whirlwind and in the storm, and the clouds are the dust of his feet.

4 He rebuketh the sea, and maketh it dry, and drieth up all the rivers: Bashan languisheth, and Carmel, and the flower of Lebanon languisheth.

5 The mountains quake at him, and the hills melt, and the earth is burned at his presence, yea, the world, and all that dwell therein.

6 Who can stand before his indignation? and who can abide in the fierceness of his anger? his fury is poured out like fire, and the rocks are thrown down by him.

7 The LORD is good, a strong hold in the day of trouble; and he knoweth them that trust in him.

8 But with an overrunning flood he will make an utter end of the place thereof, and darkness shall pursue his enemies.

9 What do ye imagine against the LORD? he will make an utter end: affliction shall not rise up the second time.

. . . . .

12 Thus saith the LORD; Though they be quiet, and likewise many, yet thus shall they be cut down, when he shall pass through. Though I have afflicted thee, I will afflict thee no more.

13 For now will I break his yoke from off thee, and will burst thy bonds in sunder.

14 And the LORD hath given a commandment concerning thee, that no more of thy name be sown: out of the house of thy gods will I cut off the graven image and the molten image: I will make thy grave; for thou art vile.

15 Behold upon the mountains the feet of him that bringeth good tidings, that publisheth peace! O Judah, keep thy solemn feasts, perform thy vows: for the wicked shall no more pass through thee; he is utterly cut off.

Focus Thought

God hates sin and will judge it both in this life and in the life to come.

Focus Verse

Nahum 1:6

Who can stand before his indignation? and who can abide in the fierceness of his anger? his fury is poured out like fire, and the rocks are thrown down by him.

47

Would a Loving God Judge Me?

by Richard M. Davis

How many times have I heard individuals ask, "Would a loving God really send someone to Hell?" Actually, as I have heard some ministers answer, it is more like "God allows them to choose that destiny." It really is about personal choice, with which God has empowered all humankind. Hell is a real, eternal destination; and many people will choose to go there by choosing to live sinful lives on earth, separated from God's will and purpose. Still, to suggest that God's love and His judgment are incompatible aspects of His nature is simply untrue. God loves us all dearly, even those who choose to exclude Him from their lives and thereby choose Hell as their final destiny.

In his article titled "Would a Loving God Judge Me?," author David Wilson writes, "So what is God like? Well, most people today would happily declare that God is love, and this is indeed a biblical description of God. . . . But that is not the whole story. The Bible tells us that God is holy. . . . When Isaiah . . . heard the angels crying 'Holy, holy, holy,' he responded by saying, 'Woe is me, for I am undone . . .' (Isaiah 6:5).

"The Bible also tells us that God is just. . . . Unfortunately, this creates a major problem . . . because if God judges us according to His righteous standard, we would all be destroyed. . . . The only way God can be just and forgive us our sins is if the penalty we deserve is borne by someone else . . ." (*http://www.waterford-assembly.com/*, accessed March 21, 2012).

Jesus Christ has paid the price for the judgment of our sins, but we must accept His gift and embrace the salvation He has provided.

I. THE CHARACTER OF GOD, THE JUDGE
  A. Jealous, Avenging, and Wrathful, Yet Slow to Anger and Great in Power
  B. Irresistible in Judgment
  C. Evidence of God's Hatred of Sin Seen in His Dealing with Nineveh
II. CERTAINTY OF THE DOOM OF NINEVEH
  A. Description of the Siege of Nineveh
  B. God's Determination to Destroy the City
III. GOD CAN TAKE AWAY SIN AND GIVE PEACE
  A. Peace Proclaimed
  B. Worship Enjoined
  C. Enemies Vanquished

Contemplating the Topic

It is interesting to learn *Nahum* means "consoler," given his message concerned the complete destruction of the vast and powerful Assyrian empire. In reality, Nahum's message was written not to warn Assyria but for the benefit of God's people. Although for more than a century the anger of God for Assyria had simmered on the back burner—turned low by His long-suffering—it soon would boil over with the heat of full-blown wrath for what the Assyrians had done to Israel. Therefore, regardless of how things seemed, God would not forget the plight of His people, for anyone who touched the apple of God's eye touched Him. (See Zechariah 2:8; Deuteronomy 32:10; Genesis 12:3.)

The capital city of Nineveh was the seat of civilization and commerce in the ancient world. Strongly fortified and magnificently wealthy, she enjoyed prestige and power but had a wide, cruel streak and possessed the same tough hide, lethal claws, and razor-sharp teeth of a vicious honey badger. To the countries who had cowered under Assyria's onslaughts, Nineveh seemed invincible.

Transparency 1

Transparency 1 shows a honey badger and says, "Nineveh was as savage as a honey badger. God determined to destroy Nineveh for her cruelty to His people and for taunting Him."

Approximately 150 years before Nahum's day, Nineveh had mourned and repented in response to the preaching of Jonah. As time passed, however, the nation quickly reverted to its heathenish practices. Soon after their response to Jonah's message, Shalmaneser V besieged Samaria and his successor, Sargon III, took the more prosperous citizens into exile and replaced them with foreigners. A few years later Sennacherib attacked Jerusalem, and if not for the intervention of God, would have destroyed it. Rampant sin and pride corrupted Assyria from the inside out. The nation was ripe for judgment.

In strongly worded and emotionally charged language, Nahum gave his audience "an audio-visual experience by means of his powerful poetic style" (C. Hassell Bullock, *An Introduction to the Old Testament Prophetic Books*, Chicago: Moody Press, 1986). He described warriors dressed in red, flashing steel, racing chariots, galloping horses, piles of corpses, and mourning women. Nahum's message to Assyria was not just a threat like Obadiah's to Edom, but it contained the "virtual reality" of imminent judgment.

Searching the Scriptures

I. THE CHARACTER OF GOD, THE JUDGE

A. Jealous, Avenging, and Wrathful, Yet Slow to Anger and Great in Power

Nahum began his narrative by opening a window to observe God from a point of view most modern Christians are not used to seeing: "God is jealous" (Nahum 1:2). In the human milieu the word "jealousy" evokes a sense of suspicion, mistrust, possessiveness, and malignity. Divine jealousy, however, transcends human jealousy. God is completely distinct from all people, all things, all false deities, and all feelings. He resides outside the boundaries of time and creation. Thus the word "jealous" as used in Nahum 1:2 perhaps would be better translated "zealous." God is jealous over many things, but especially His deity, His sovereignty, and His own people.

1. *God is jealous over His deity.* "Thou shalt have no other gods before me" (Exodus 20:3). The first commandment is not an admission of the existence of other gods, but an oft-repeated declaration that He is God and "there is none else" (Isaiah 45:22). He alone should be worshiped.

2. *God is jealous over His sovereignty.* "Unto me every knee shall bow, every tongue shall swear" (Isaiah 45:23). (See Philippians 2:10-11.) As Creator, God has the right to command us. God said, "Remember these, O Jacob and Israel; . . . I have formed thee; thou art my servant: . . . Thus saith the LORD, thy redeemer, and he that formed thee from the

womb, I am the LORD that maketh all things" (Isaiah 44:21, 24).

3. *God is jealous over His own people.* He wants their trust, their companionship, their loyalty, and their love. His jealousy compels Him to carefully and consistently watch over them. Jesus mourned over His people's rejection of His care: "O Jerusalem, Jerusalem . . . how often would I have gathered thy children together, even as a hen gathereth her chickens under her wings, and ye would not!" (Matthew 23:37). (See Psalm 91:4.)

Another aspect of God's care for His people is His vengeance and wrath toward anyone who harms them.

"The LORD revengeth, and is furious; the LORD will take vengeance on his adversaries, and he reserveth wrath for his enemies . . . and will not at all acquit the wicked" (Nahum 1:2-3).

When Sennacherib sent a letter sneering at God's powerlessness to deliver Judah, Hezekiah took the letter to the house of the Lord and prayed. Isaiah assured Hezekiah of the Lord's contempt for the Assyrian king: "Whereas thou hast prayed to me against Sennacherib king of Assyria: This is the word which the LORD hath spoken concerning him: . . . Because thy [Sennacherib's] rage against me, and thy tumult, is come up into mine ears, therefore will I put my hook in thy nose, and my bridle in thy lips, and I will turn thee back by the way by which thou camest. . . . the zeal of the LORD of hosts shall do this" (Isaiah 37:21, 29, 32). Not even Assyria could withstand the wrath of God.

Assyria was a den of lions. The lions had savaged Mesopotamia, tearing, strangling, and filling their den with prey. God said, "Behold, I am against thee" (Nahum 2:13). Once God has turned His face against a people, certain doom awaits.

B. Irresistible in Judgment

Nahum expressed harshly the certainty of God's crushing judgment upon Nineveh, a colossal city that stretched for thirty miles along the eastern bank of the Tigris River. It was protected by a broad one-hundred-foot-high wall and defended by fifteen hundred towers. Yet God's judgment soon would overwhelm the city like an overflowing flood. The psalmist said, "The wicked shall be turned into hell, and all the nations that forget God" (Psalm 9:17).

Transparency 2 includes some words and phrases describing the multifaceted character of God.

Even in the midst of this tidal wave of judgment Nahum offered hope to those who trust in God.

"The LORD is good, a strong hold in the day of trouble; and he knoweth them that trust in him" (Nahum 1:7).

Although we are in this world, we are not of the world. Like a lily growing in the midst of a swamp, the church stands forth pure and white—a beacon of hope displaying God's mercy to all. Although we as Christians have been criticized, ostracized, and maybe even brutalized by the world, the Word tells us to lift up our heads, for our redemption draws nigh. Thus, we discover this truth: while God vents His wrath upon sinners, He simultaneously blesses those who trust in Him.

Although we are in this world, we are not of the world.

C. Evidence of God's Hatred of Sin Seen in His Dealing with Nineveh

Many nonbelievers hold to the misconception that God's goodness prevents Him from becoming angry and destructive when His laws are violated. But the Bible gives evidence to the contrary.

"Behold, all souls are mine . . . the soul that sinneth, it shall die" (Ezekiel 18:4).

In the case of Nineveh, Nahum prophesied the nation would reap the same harsh and merciless treatment it had meted out to those they conquered. "But with an overrunning flood he will make an utter end of the place" (Nahum 1:8-9). Mankind should learn a lesson from Nineveh. God will judge sinners, and godless nations will disappear from the face of the earth.

II. CERTAINTY OF THE DOOM OF NINEVEH

Judgment came upon Nineveh because the people were vile (Nahum 1:14); they were full of murder, strife, lies, violence, and extortion. When the cup of iniquity is full, God pours out His wrath and there is no remedy.

A. Description of the Siege of Nineveh

God began His diatribe against Nineveh with mockery. He told them to fortify the wall, store ammunition, watch, and get ready. Yet it would all be in vain because someone was coming who would dash them in pieces in spite of all their fortifications and munitions.

Judgment began when a Medo-Babylonian coalition besieged Nineveh for two years, but with little initial success. Nineveh's warriors repelled them and inflicted heavy losses. However, as Nineveh celebrated their victory with carousing and reveling, the besiegers took advantage and drove the Assyrians behind their walls. They cut off a portion of the troops and pushed them into the river.

"The gates of the rivers shall be opened" (Nahum 2:6).

The third year of the siege arrived, along with heavy rains. Dams broke and the system of canals opened up, flooding the city and leaving it standing in a lake. The swift and powerful current carried away a portion of the wall, giving the besiegers an entrance. No one came to help Assyria, for the nation had alienated their neighbors by reneging on promises to join in their battles.

B. God's Determination to Destroy the City

"The palace shall be dissolved" (Nahum 2:6).

Archeologists have unearthed numerous palaces in ancient Nineveh, many of them showing evidence of being destroyed by fire: calcined alabaster, charred wood, and colossal statues split through with heat. Flood and fire destroyed temples, palaces, royal tombs, and shrines. The king, recognizing imminent death, gathered together his concubines and eunuchs, and mounting a funeral pyre, perished in the flames. Looters carried away treasures, and several thousand people who could not escape to Assyrian strongholds were either massacred or deported out of the city.

III. GOD CAN TAKE AWAY SIN AND GIVE PEACE

God does not watch and wait for a person to sin so He can hurl His wrath upon him. In fact, it is quite the opposite. The stories of Nineveh and of Israel's history teach us God delays judgment because He is "not willing that any should perish" II Peter 3:9).

Transparency 3

Transparency 3 quotes portions of Ezekiel 33:11 and Romans 5:8.

"Say unto them, As I live, saith the Lord GOD, I have no pleasure in the death of the wicked; but that the wicked turn from his way and live: turn ye, turn ye from your evil ways; for why will ye die, O house of Israel?" (Ezekiel 33:11).

Someone might rightly ask, "How could God ever want me? I've been a sinner all my life." The answer is, He came seeking us first.

"God commendeth his love toward us, in that, while we were yet sinners, Christ died for us" (Romans 5:8).

God loves sinners, but He will not tolerate sin. Thus He seeks out sinful individuals and offers mercy and forgiveness to them like a king extending a golden scepter. Esther took a huge risk when she came unbidden into the court of King Ahasuerus, but when he saw her he favored her and extended the golden scepter, saying, "What wilt thou, queen Esther? and what is thy request? It shall be even given thee to the half of the kingdom" (Esther 5:3). Likewise, sinners cannot approach the throne of Jesus Christ unless the Father draws them (John 6:44). God's mercy and love woo the sinner to an altar of repentance where he can receive forgiveness, restoration, and a spiritual inheritance. (See Daniel 9:9; I Corinthians 6:11.)

Nahum encouraged the Israelite captives in the grip of Nineveh's cruel bondage that there was still hope in the midst of trouble. In their despair, they should not forget God was still on His throne. If they continued to serve the

Lord, He would come to deliver them and pour out judgment on Nineveh. (See Nahum 1:15.)

A. Peace Proclaimed

The Lord will always send someone to proclaim the glorious good news prior to judgment. Indeed, "how beautiful upon the mountains are the feet of him that bringeth good tidings, that publisheth peace; that bringeth good tidings of good, that publisheth salvation; that saith unto Zion, Thy God reigneth!" (Isaiah 52:7). The purpose of the gospel is to purge the individual's soul and spirit, dispel doubts, and bring peace to his heart. Where sin had fostered confusion, hatred, and strife, God now delivers him from every evil work and grants him an inheritance in the heavenly kingdom of Jesus Christ. (See II Timothy 4:18).

We can praise our Lord Jesus Christ for giving us victory over our enemy and our past.

B. Worship Enjoined

As we drink from the cup of salvation, the Lord replaces our spirit of heaviness with a garment of praise and replaces our mourning with joy. Beauty arises out of the ashes of our ruined lives. (See Isaiah 61:3.) Thank God for His mercy and grace! Like Israel watching their Egyptian oppressors perish in the waters of the Red Sea, we can praise our Lord Jesus Christ for giving us victory over our enemy and our past. The song "My Tribute" expresses thanks to the Redeemer.

With His blood He has saved me.
With His power He has raised me.
To God be the glory for the things He hath done.

C. Enemies Vanquished

When a person is released from the dominion of Satan and is adopted into God's family, he joins the winning side. The power of the Holy Ghost guarantees victory over sin.

1. All our sins are forgiven. (See Psalm 103:2-4; Colossians 2:13-14.)

51

2. God gives us power to tread upon our enemies. (See Psalm 44:4-7; Romans 6:14; Ephesians 1:19-23.)

3. Death cannot keep us from God's presence. (See Romans 6:23; I Corinthians 15:20-26.)

God assures, "All things work together for good to them that love God, to them who are the called according to his purpose" (Romans 8:28). Everything that happens in a believer's life is in the sovereign hand of God. God uses what happens throughout the whole range of life's experiences—whether sorrow or joy, defeat or victory, sickness or health—to work toward a good end. All of these things help us to conform to the image of his Son (Romans 8:29) whose power can make us "more than conquerors" (Romans 8:37).

"And we know that all things work together for good to them that love God, to them who are the called according to his purpose" (Romans 8:28).

Internalizing the Message

Paul said, "Behold therefore the goodness and severity of God: on them which fell, severity; but toward thee, goodness, if thou continue in his goodness: otherwise thou also shalt be cut off" (Romans 11:22). God is not, as some perceive Him, a one-dimensional character whose emotions are limited to positive ones such as love, compassion, or pleasure. Just like human beings who are created in His image, God has a wide range of personality traits and can express many emotions, both positive and negative. The Scriptures provide countless examples of God's feelings: mercy and judgment, pleasure and displeasure, joy and sorrow, meekness and wrath.

In the first chapter of Nahum, we view both sides of the character of God. He is slow to anger and great in power but will not acquit the wicked (1:3). He is good and a stronghold in the day of trouble for those who trust in Him (1:7). On the other hand, the wicked cannot stand before the fierceness of His anger, for He will pour out His fury like fire (1:6). God vents His wrath upon sinners while simultaneously blessing those who trust in Him.

The choices we make will determine which face of God we see in eternity.

REFLECTIONS

- Discuss the evidence given in Scripture that God hates sin, and that every person will have to account for his sins.
- Using the messages of Jonah and Nahum, discuss the truth found in Nahum 1:3 that God is slow to anger and just in His judgments.
- God said, "Is not my way equal?" (Ezekiel 18:25). Discuss the balance between the judgment and mercy of God.
- Many people today in both the religious and secular worlds believe that because God is love, He does not have the capability of becoming angry or destructive. Discuss.
- Discuss ways to give a message of hope to someone who asks, "How could God love me or want me? My sins are too many."

Habakkuk—Trembling, Yet Trusting

8
week of
07.21.13

Lesson Text

Habakkuk 3:3-13

3 God came from Teman, and the Holy One from mount Paran. Selah. His glory covered the heavens, and the earth was full of his praise.

4 And his brightness was as the light; he had horns coming out of his hand: and there was the hiding of his power.

5 Before him went the pestilence, and burning coals went forth at his feet.

6 He stood, and measured the earth: he beheld, and drove asunder the nations; and the everlasting mountains were scattered, the perpetual hills did bow: his ways are everlasting.

7 I saw the tents of Cushan in affliction: and the curtains of the land of Midian did tremble.

8 Was the LORD displeased against the rivers? was thine anger against the rivers? was thy wrath against the sea, that thou didst ride upon thine horses and thy chariots of salvation?

9 Thy bow was made quite naked, according to the oaths of the tribes, even thy word. Selah. Thou didst cleave the earth with rivers.

10 The mountains saw thee, and they trembled: the overflowing of the water passed by: the deep uttered his voice, and lifted up his hands on high.

11 The sun and moon stood still in their habitation: at the light of thine arrows they went, and at the shining of thy glittering spear.

12 Thou didst march through the land in indignation, thou didst thresh the heathen in anger.

13 Thou wentest forth for the salvation of thy people, even for salvation with thine anointed; thou woundedst the head out of the house of the wicked, by discovering the foundation unto the neck. Selah.

Focus Thought

In the midst of terrible circumstances we can trust God, and He will prove worthy of our trust.

Focus Verses

Habakkuk 3:17-18

Although the fig tree shall not blossom, neither shall fruit be in the vines; the labour of the olive shall fail, and the fields shall yield no meat; the flock shall be cut off from the fold, and there shall be no herd in the stalls: yet I will rejoice in the LORD, I will joy in the God of my salvation.

53

I'll Praise You in This Storm

by Dorsey Burk

Perhaps for the first time in my life, the scenario Habakkuk described in 3:17 seems like a real possibility. Friends have declared bankruptcy and lost their homes. People in our local assembly have been out of work, and their bills continue to pile up. Drought has dried up crops in Texas while floods have washed away the harvest in the South.

I know there's talk about the economy improving, and the stock market is doing better. But will they continue to improve in this volatile political season? I just don't know what to expect.

As I write, gasoline prices are fluttering at $4.00 a gallon, but that probably will go up when St. Louisans are required to use the more expensive summer blends. My wife tells me of big increases in food prices. Another local company announced today it will be laying off over four hundred people. The future is frightening in many respects.

What can we do? Habakkuk offers the only viable alternative to wringing our hands. We are to praise God in spite of our circumstances. Marc Hall of Casting Crowns wrote,

I'll praise You in this storm
And I will lift my hands
For You are who You are
No matter where I am.

Yes, life is tough. It may get tougher before the church is raptured. But God is still God no matter where in life we may be. My economic woes, my emotional lows, and my physical aches and pains do not lessen the power, might, and majesty of almighty God. So I'm going to face life's storms and rejoice in the Lord because I know He's still God.

I. THE PROPHET'S PERPLEXITY
  A. The Lord's Reply
  B. Habakkuk's Question of God's Choice
II. GOD'S ANSWER
  A. Habakkuk Awaits God's Answer
  B. God's Instructions to Habakkuk
  C. The Just Shall Live by Faith
  D. Catalog of the Babylonians'
    (Chaldeans') Sins
  E. Silence before the Storm of God's Judgment
III. HABAKKUK'S PRAYER AND TRUST
  A. Habakkuk's Appeal to God to Act
    for His People
  B. Habakkuk's Review of God's Care
    for Israel from Egypt to Canaan
  C. Habakkuk's Waiting for the Enemy
    to Be Punished
  D. Habakkuk's Trust in God
IV. OUR CHOICE TODAY
  TO TRUST AND PRAISE GOD

Contemplating the Topic

People who trust God will never question His plans—or will they? One short but significant book in the Bible is full of such questioning. The Book of Habakkuk is a back-and-forth conversation between a prophet and God. It begins with Habakkuk's complaint about the wickedness of God's people. The Lord responded that He would judge His people by using the Chaldeans, a "bitter and hasty nation," the "terrible and dreadful" Chaldeans. (See Habakkuk 1:6-7.) Habakkuk did not think that appropriate and told God so. God answered Habakkuk's protests, but His pronouncements brought no comfort. This presented Habakkuk with a dilemma. He could choose to live in anger and fear, or he could embrace trust in God. It is just this sort of choice that is presented to every one of us today.

Searching the Scriptures

I. THE PROPHET'S PERPLEXITY

Habakkuk's world was a very confusing place. Enemies of the Jewish people abounded both inside and out. Judah had become a poor and weak nation, smaller by far than at any other time in its history. Nineveh had fallen in

612 BC, but the Assyrian Empire, though declining, was still a force to be reckoned with, especially because of its alliance with Egypt. Carchemish was one of the last strongholds of Assyria, and the Babylonians and Medes were on their way to subdue it.

Egypt wanted to prevent this at all costs. But as they hurried along the Way of the Sea to Carchemish, they encountered King Josiah's army at Megiddo on the plain of Jezreel. King Necho tried to talk peace with Josiah, but the Judean king would not listen. A battle ensued and Josiah was killed. (See II Kings 23:29-30; II Chronicles 35:20-25.) Egypt won at Megiddo but lost at Carchemish.

Besides the external enemies, there were problems among God's people. Although there had been a revival during Josiah's reign, God was still angry about the ungodliness that had flourished during the reign of Manasseh (II Kings 23:26-27) when he had "seduced them [Judah] to do more evil than did the nations whom the LORD destroyed before the children of Israel" (II Kings 21:9). In Habakkuk's day, toward the end of Josiah's reign, the powerful oppressed the powerless and integrity waned while corruption increased. Habakkuk had tried to stem the tide of evil by calling the people to repentance, but no one heeded him and evil still flourished. He complained, "O LORD, how long shall I cry, and thou wilt not hear!" (Habakkuk 1:2).

A. The Lord's Reply

God always hears our prayers and God always answers prayer, though it may not be according to our timetable, and we may not like the answers the Lord gives. This was the case with Habakkuk. God answered the prophet's complaint by revealing His plan to use the godless Chaldeans (Babylonians) to judge the Jewish people. They would destroy the land, wreaking havoc on the rich and poor, the good and bad. Habakkuk was stunned.

Some responses seem more unfair than the problem they are addressing. If two children are fighting over a toy, a mother may teach them a lesson by taking the toy away from both of them. From a child's perspective, this is a bad solution. It is almost impossible for a child to understand things from an adult perspective. If it is difficult for a child to grasp an adult perspective, how much more difficult is it for us to understand God's perspective.

God showed Habakkuk a vivid picture of the judgment He would unleash upon His people. With horses swifter than leopards and destruction swooping in like an eagle (1:8), the Babylonians would attack and possess even the strongholds of Judah, destroying the most powerful (1:10). They would possess the homes throughout the entire breadth of the land (1:6). While it was not altogether clear when such destruction would take place, Habakkuk understood that the fulfillment would be very soon; indeed, most scholars suggest God's pronouncements to Habakkuk were fulfilled within a few decades.

Habakkuk's knowledge of the pride and godlessness of the Chaldeans (1:11) made it difficult to accept God's intention to use them to punish the people of God. He knew the Babylonians would credit their god Bel with their successful campaign throughout Judea. Habakkuk could not fathom how God could allow it. Habakkuk had petitioned God to intervene because of the wickedness of the Jewish people, but he did not expect this sort of intervention!

B. Habakkuk's Question of God's Choice

One common misconception is that a person who really loves the Lord will not question God's wisdom. However, along with the psalmists who often queried God's actions and purposes, Habakkuk dared to voice his own set of questions. God's answer shocked the prophet and he burst out in protest. Surely God did not intend to destroy His own people. It simply did not seem to be right. He challenged God, "We shall not die" (1:12). Habakkuk reminded God of His character and faithfulness (1:12). He asked how Jehovah could possibly punish the Jewish people with an enemy that was certainly less righteous than they.

"Wherefore lookest thou upon them that deal treacherously, and holdest thy tongue when the wicked devoureth the man that is more righteous than he?" (Habakkuk 1:13).

Transparency 1

Transparency 1 shows a net of fish and states, "Habakkuk complained the helpless Jews were like fish caught in a net, gloated over by wicked fishermen."

Habakkuk used a simile to describe the helplessness of the Jewish people against this ruthless destroyer. They were like fish of the sea caught in a net and gloated over by the wicked fishermen (1:14-17).

II. GOD'S ANSWER

It does not seem right that wicked people prosper, particularly at times when those who are faithfully living for God are struggling. Such circumstances run counter to what we believe ought to be, even to what we believe the Word of God promises. For instance, the Book of Proverbs assures blessings to those who do right, to those who are living in covenant. One proverb teaches, "The blessing of the LORD, it maketh rich, and he addeth no sorrow with it" (Proverbs 10:22). It is no wonder Habakkuk had questions.

Yet it is important to understand that God sees things differently than we do. Sometimes when we focus on our difficult circumstances, we forget God can use even terrible circumstances for good. While it boggled Habakkuk's mind that God could accomplish His purpose through a godless people, He could begin to understand only when He acknowledged that God's perspective is bigger than any human understanding. In chapter two of Habakkuk God began to offer hope; yet it was a hope that would unfold in time.

A. Habakkuk Awaits God's Answer

The scope of Habakkuk's concern encompassed not just his own future but the future existence of Judah. As a prophet, he played an important role, one similar to a watchman on the wall of a city. In the ancient Near East, watchmen stationed in a city's watchtowers scanned the horizon for anyone who approached, whether friend or foe. Habakkuk wrote, "I will stand upon my watch, and set me upon the tower, and will watch to see what [God] will say unto me" (2:1). Habakkuk was not sure what God's response would be to his objection of the divine sentence of judgment; nevertheless, he awaited God's correction and thought about how he would answer God's reproof (2:1).

B. God's Instructions to Habakkuk

During Habakkuk's sojourn in the watchtower, God's promise to deliver His people from the Babylonians renewed hope in the prophet's heart. God told Habakkuk to write the message of hope so anyone who read it would understand and run to spread the good news (2:2).

But the message did not end there. It is still true today that God cannot deliver His people unless there is something to deliver them from. Before He could deliver Israel from Egypt, Israel had to move there and become enslaved. Before God could deliver the Jews from certain death in Media Persia, Haman had to devise a wicked plot to annihilate them. Before God could deliver Judah from Nebuchadnezzar, the Babylonians first had to invade, destroy, plunder, kill, and take captives. But if Judah would cling to God's vision of hope, they could trust God's promise to deliver.

C. The Just Shall Live by Faith

As we have already discovered in Habakkuk, when evil attacks, it is not always the guilty alone who suffer. Indeed, those who live for the Lord often endure the same hardships as the guilty. Yet, it is interesting to see the different ways people respond to suffering. According to principles from the Book of Habakkuk, the proud respond to calamity by trusting in themselves; this is not helpful because their moral character is not upright (2:4).

On the other hand, those who are living godly lives demonstrate this by trusting in the God who called them into covenant. The principle offered in Habakkuk 2:4 is a key principle in life. "The just shall live"—that is, they will survive, endure, make it to the end—through their faithful living in covenant relationship with God, regardless of what comes against them. The spiritual truth "the just shall live by faith" is just as true today as it ever has been.

Transparency 2

Transparency 2 quotes a portion of Hebrews 10:38.

D. Catalog of the Babylonians' (Chaldeans') Sins

God did not need Habakkuk to point out the evils of Babylon. As if to say, "Thank you, Habakkuk, but I already know how evil they are," the Lord repeated Habakkuk's list of evils and even added a few the prophet had missed. He depicted the Babylonians as a drinking man hungrily swallowing nations and peoples (2:5).

Judah should not lose hope, however, for God would repay Babylon in kind for the evil they had done. God instructed those who had suffered to prophetically sing a "taunt-song" against them (*New American Standard*); that is, a derisive song of judgment against the Babylonian. God proclaimed, "Take up a parable against him, and a taunting proverb against him" (Habakkuk 2:6).

The rest of chapter two declares in haunting poetry how Babylon would be destroyed. "Because you [Babylon] have plundered many nations, all the remnant of the people shall plunder you, because of men's blood and the violence of the land and the city, and of all who dwell in it" (Habakkuk 2:8, NKJV). The very stones of the walls and support beams would cry out against the Babylonian for his evil (2:11).

Though the Babylonians would think their gods had given them victory over the Jewish people, this was hardly the case. Their victory was in vain, for there will come a day when "the earth shall be filled with the knowledge of the glory of the LORD" (2:14). Jehovah prophesied His victory would be as total as the way in which the water covers the bottom of the sea (2:14).

E. Silence before the Storm of God's Judgment

Babylonian ritual in homage to their god Bel was among the most elaborate religious rituals in the entire ancient Near East. Procession and pomp were the norm in Babylonian worship. Elaborate gold-covered idols sat in shrines that extended high above the earth. Parades and pronouncements declared that all their wealth and beauty was dedicated to the Babylonian pantheon. The very pervasiveness of the religion and politics of Babylon seemed to prove the superiority of their religious system and of their gods.

Yet Jehovah declared to Habakkuk that these man-made symbols proved nothing. These so-called "gods" were not gods at all; they were merely crafted images that could never speak (2:18). The foolish Babylonians prayed to inanimate objects they created with their own hands (2:19).

In contrast, there is only one real God who speaks and declares; one who prophesies and it comes to pass. Jehovah alone had power to pronounce judgment upon Babylon (2:6-19), and because He was God, it would come to pass. The Jewish people should not be intimidated by false worship, for "the LORD is in his holy temple" (2:20). Indeed, when the glory and majesty of the work of God is ultimately revealed, worshipers of false gods will be speechless. Appropriately, Habakkuk closed this section with the pronouncement, "Let all the earth keep silence before Him" (2:20).

III. HABAKKUK'S PRAYER AND TRUST

Habakkuk closes with a song that encompasses God's promises and the response of His people. Habakkuk 3:1 indicates that Habakkuk's prayer was "upon Shigionoth." This phrase is the same sort of preface as is offered in Psalm 7, and while there is a question whether this has to do with the sort of instrument or song being performed, it is clear the chapter is a song, one that captures the celebration of trust embraced by Habakkuk. In the song, the prophet offered reasons why God's people should live faithful lives.

A. Habakkuk's Appeal to God to Act for His People

Habakkuk began the psalm by considering God's miraculous power in establishing Israel as a nation. He requested another miracle, that God would "revive thy work in the midst of the years" (3:2). That is, Habakkuk wanted God to work with Judah in the same way He delivered Israel from Egypt to create a people.

B. Habakkuk's Review of God's Care for Israel from Egypt to Canaan

Given the poetic nature of the song, it is sometimes hard to ascertain what Habakkuk was celebrating because He often referred to names and events indirectly or in repetitious ways. Nevertheless, the psalm powerfully emphasizes the greatness of God and His work.

The psalm begins by standing in the perspective of Israel as they experienced the glory of God on Mount Sinai (Exodus 19:16). "Teman" and "Paran" are poetically parallel to Mount Sinai; thus, Habakkuk celebrated this Sinai experience by singing, "God came from Teman, and the Holy One from mount Paran" (Habakkuk 3:3), a repetition that celebrated the giving of the Law on Sinai. Further, God's glory was experienced as "light" and "horns," or rays of light that came from His hand (3:4).

Given the mighty demonstration of Jehovah's glory at Sinai, it was easy for Habakkuk to reflect backward from Mount Sinai to Israel's deliverance from Egyptian slavery and to project forward to God's deliverance as Israel made ready to possess the Promised Land. Because Jehovah "descended upon [Mount Sinai] in fire" (Exodus 19:18), Habakkuk wrote that "burning coals went forth at his feet" and "before him went the pestilence" (Habakkuk 3:5).

In a poetic description of God's going forth from Sinai, the psalm of Habakkuk proclaims Jehovah "drove asunder the nations,"and the "mountains were scattered"; in a poetic repetition Habakkuk saw "the tents of Cushan in affliction: and the curtains of Midian did tremble" (Habakkuk 3:6-7).

Subsequent verses poetically celebrate God's marching into Canaan as He led His people to victory. Habakkuk had both the Red Sea and the Jordan River in view when he sang of God's anger with the rivers and the sea as He divided them (3:8). He said God's "bow was made quite naked" (3:9), meaning He unsheathed it and filled its string with arrows.

In verses 10-11, Habakkuk poetically represented nature as viewing God's victorious power. Mountains trembled in response as the waters separated and "the deep uttered his voice, and lifted up his hands on high." The sun and the moon stood still in response to God's arrows and spear.

The psalm was more about God's deliverance from His people's enemies than it was about Israel's victories. God had been at work in their conquest. God threshed (by trampling) the nations (3:12); He wounded the neck of the wicked (3:13) and "with his staves" pierced "the head of his villages" (3:14). Further, the real reason the Red Sea parted and piled up (Exodus 14:22) was the Lord "didst walk through the sea with thine horses" (Habakkuk 3:15).

C. Habakkuk's Waiting for the Enemy to Be Punished

Despite God's great power, He still would allow judgment to come upon the Jewish people. Things would get worse before they got better. In verse 16, Habakkuk reflected on the prophecy that was delivered to him by the Lord. Poetically, he mourned with personal grief as it related to the coming judgment, trembling with a sense of inner decay. Yet, because of God's power and might, he confessed he would "rest"—quietly wait on God's provision—"in the day of trouble." Thus, the invasion of the Babylonians would not be merely a one-sided judgment. Jehovah promised He would "invade them with his troops." Ultimately, God would bring victory.

D. Habakkuk's Trust in God

Habakkuk was not altogether sure how God would bring ultimate deliverance, but he was sure God would triumph in the end. Consequently, Habakkuk offered the only appropri-ate response to this "in-between time," the time when he could do nothing but patiently await God's deliverance: Habakkuk offered praise. Indeed, the Book of Habakkuk closes with this affirmation of trust.

Transparency 3 pictures a fig tree and quotes portions of Habakkuk 3:17-18.

In verse 17, Habakkuk professed that whether or not he had any physical evidence of God's blessing, it would not make a difference to his faith. If the fig tree did not blossom, if there were no grapes on the vines or olives harvested from the trees, or even if the flock offered no yield, Habakkuk's response would still be the same. He pronounced, "Yet I will rejoice in the LORD, I will joy in the God of my salvation" (3:18).

Habakkuk had confidence God would be with him no matter what. Just as God enables a deer or a mountain goat to tread with confidence on uncertain and treacherous trails, so Habakkuk offered in celebration, "The LORD God is my strength, and he will make my feet like hinds' feet, and he will make me to walk upon mine high places" (3:19).

We can choose to praise God in the face of adversity.

IV. OUR CHOICE TODAY TO TRUST AND PRAISE GOD

We live in uncertain times. Just as in Habakkuk's day, we often find injustice where we expect integrity. To make matters worse, we cannot always find recourse for wrongs that have been done. Such times compel us to place our trust in One who never fails. Just as Habakkuk had a choice to doubt or to affirm his trust in God, we also have that same choice today. Further, just as Habakkuk expressed his confidence in God by a song of praise, we too can choose to praise God in the face of adversity.

Internalizing the Message

New Testament writers drew assurance from the words of Habakkuk, and we can too. The writer of Hebrews addressed those who were in very confusing circumstances to stand firm and not to cast away their confidence. Drawing from the thematic prophecy of Habakkuk, he wrote that the coming of the Lord—God's deliverance—was certain, citing, "For yet a little while, and he that shall come will come, and will not tarry. Now the just shall live by faith" (Hebrews 10:37-38, which alludes to Habakkuk 2:3-4). Our times echo the uncertainty of the age when Hebrews was written. We too can place our hope in Jesus Christ by holding on to the one thing that is certain: God's promise of redemption.

When Jews opposed Paul in Antioch, he reminded them of Habakkuk's promise of judgment upon the Jewish people who did wrong (Acts 13:41, citing Habakkuk 1:5). Paul was certainly disappointed when the people he thought would receive his words turned against him.

Yet Paul is not the only one who has ever been disappointed. Betrayals happen more than we care to admit. Those upon whom we have depended sometimes disappoint us in very tangible ways. It is at these times we too can draw from Paul's faith in the promises of Habakkuk. While betrayal and wickedness might be resident even among those who should know better, the promises of God will stand. The just shall live by their faithfulness.

Sometimes we believe that because we are living for the Lord, everything ought to work out really well. Yet, instead of things getting better after we pray, they seem to get worse. It is then we can choose the same solution as Habakkuk. We can decide that our faith does not depend upon outward blessings; it depends upon the character and power of God. Even though we do not always see the answers to our difficulties, we can choose to praise God and wait on the answers only He can give.

REFLECTIONS

- Discuss appropriate/inappropriate ways and times to question God.
- When we question God or ask Him to right a wrong, His answer is not always what we expect. Discuss.
- Hebrews 12:6 says, "For whom the Lord loveth he chasteneth, and scourgeth every son whom he receiveth." Like Habakkuk, it is hard not to question the justifiability of what or whom God uses to chasten us. Discuss.
- During times of chastisement, a believer does well to remember past victories and deliverance God has wrought in his life. Discuss.
- Habakkuk said, "The just shall live by his faith." Discuss.

9
week of
07.28.13

Zephaniah—Hope

Zephaniah 3:8-16, 18-20

8 Therefore wait ye upon me, saith the LORD, until the day that I rise up to the prey: for my determination is to gather the nations, that I may assemble the kingdoms, to pour upon them mine indignation, even all my fierce anger: for all the earth shall be devoured with the fire of my jealousy.

9 For then will I turn to the people a pure language, that they may all call upon the name of the LORD, to serve him with one consent.

10 From beyond the rivers of Ethiopia my suppliants, even the daughter of my dispersed, shall bring mine offering.

11 In that day shalt thou not be ashamed for all thy doings, wherein thou hast transgressed against me: for then I will take away out of the midst of thee them that rejoice in thy pride, and thou shalt no more be haughty because of my holy mountain.

12 I will also leave in the midst of thee an afflicted and poor people, and they shall trust in the name of the LORD.

13 The remnant of Israel shall not do iniquity, nor speak lies; neither shall a deceitful tongue be found in their mouth: for they shall feed and lie down, and none shall make them afraid.

14 Sing, O daughter of Zion; shout, O Israel; be glad and rejoice with all the heart, O daughter of Jerusalem.

15 The LORD hath taken away thy judgments, he hath cast out thine enemy: the king of Israel, even the LORD, is in the midst of thee: thou shalt not see evil any more.

16 In that day it shall be said to Jerusalem, Fear thou not: and to Zion, Let not thine hands be slack.

. . . . .

18 I will gather them that are sorrowful for the solemn assembly, who are of thee, to whom the reproach of it was a burden.

19 Behold, at that time I will undo all that afflict thee: and I will save her that halteth, and gather her that was driven out; and I will get them praise and fame in every land where they have been put to shame.

20 At that time will I bring you again, even in the time that I gather you: for I will make you a name and a praise among all people of the earth, when I turn back your captivity before your eyes, saith the LORD.

Focus Thought

God has to deal with sin, but never does God leave the sinner without hope. He will save all who will repent.

Focus Verse

Zephaniah 3:17

The LORD thy God in the midst of thee is mighty; he will save, he will rejoice over thee with joy; he will rest in his love, he will joy over thee with singing.

Hope for the Hopeless
by Dorsey Burk

Looking at the economic, social, and political chaos that abounds, life offers little hope in this world. A headline caught my eye, but I refused to read the article for fear it would depress me. I look at my grandchildren and wonder what kind of world they will inherit.

But then I remember that my hope is where it has always been. David said, "Why art thou cast down, O my soul? and why art thou disquieted within me? hope thou in God: for I shall yet praise him, who is the health of my countenance, and my God" (Psalm 42:11). The only hope I have ever had has been in God alone.

Jesus Christ is the only hope for a world wallowing in sin. Psychology may offer a cause for the neurosis. Law enforcement may restrain the criminal. Social programs may care for victims, addicts, and the needy. But Jesus Christ is the only One who can forgive sin, put the pieces of a broken life back together, and turn tragedy into beauty.

The Word of God indicates that conditions in our world will only get worse. Second Timothy 3:13 states, "But evil men and seducers shall wax worse and worse, deceiving, and being deceived." Yet David said, "For in the time of trouble he shall hide me in his pavilion: in the secret of his tabernacle shall he hide me; he shall set me up upon a rock" (Psalm 27:5).

Let's anchor our hope in the Rock of Ages.

I. GOD'S DETERMINATION
   TO EXECUTE JUDGMENT
   A. On All the Earth
   B. On Judah and Jerusalem because of Idolatry
   C. The Day of the Lord under the Figure
      of a Sacrifice
   D. The Terror of the Day of the Lord
II. JUDAH CALLED TO REPENT
III. THE DOOM OF GENTILE NATIONS
   A. The Philistines
   B. The Moabites and Ammonites
   C. The Ethiopians
   D. The Assyrians and the City of Nineveh
IV. WOE PRONOUNCED ON JERUSALEM
   A. Jerusalem's Sins
   B. Greed of the Princes and the Judges
   C. Levity and Treachery of the Prophets
      and Sacrilege of the Priests
   D. The Lord's Presence in Judgment
V. MESSAGE OF HOPE
   TO THE FAITHFUL REMNANT
   A. Destruction of Wicked Gentiles
   B. Conversion of the Remaining Nations
   C. Restoration of Dispersed Israel
   D. Rejoicing over the Second Advent of Christ

Contemplating the Topic

"If anyone wishes all the secret oracles of the prophets to be given in a brief compendium, let him read through this brief Zephaniah."—Martin Bucer (1528)

Zephaniah prophesied during the reign of King Josiah, the last of the godly kings of Judah. Zephaniah was of royal lineage, King Hezekiah being his great-great-grandfather. Presumably, this kinship gave him direct access to the ear of the boy king. (Josiah was eight years old when he became king of Judah.) It is possible the prophet had a positive spiritual influence upon Josiah, who, in contrast to his father Amon (II Kings 21:19-24), diligently sought after the Lord, cleansed the land of idolatry, and repaired the Temple of Solomon.

Desiring to turn Judah back to monotheistic worship of Jehovah, Josiah in the eighteenth year of his reign ordered the repairing of the Temple. During the renovation, Hilkiah, the high priest, discovered the book of the Law and gave it to Shaphan, a scribe, who took it to the king's court and read it to the king. Josiah rent his garments for fear that Judah had transgressed to the point God would destroy them (II Kings 22:11-13).

It is probable Zephaniah's ministry greatly influenced the revival that came about during Josiah's reign, for the prophet spoke against the same evils King Josiah purged from Israel. Zephaniah's mention of Assyria and omission of Babylon provide a time frame for his writing of about 630 BC. He prophesied against Judah and Jerusalem as well as other nations around them, saying if they did not repent they would face the consequences of the impending judgment of God. Yet during his pronouncement of the Day of Judgment, he seasoned his sermon with hope that restoration would surely come.

Unfortunately, the revival during Josiah's reign was short lived; and soon after, the Babylonians came and destroyed, slaughtered, looted, and carried away thousands of captives to Babylon. (See II Kings 24:11-25:21.)

Searching the Scriptures

I. GOD'S DETERMINATION TO EXECUTE JUDGMENT

A. On All the Earth

The word "remnant" in announcements of judgment emphasized two things: (1) the totality of God's judgment, whether on non-Israelites or Israelites; and (2) the element of God's abiding grace and mercy. In some cases God may have emphasized the complete and total elimination of a people—that no trace or remnant would remain after the dust settled. On the other hand, in some cases God specifically promised that a remnant of His people would remain after the judgment was complete.

Since His covenant people had desecrated the holiness of God by adopting the false deities and the wickedness of surrounding nations, God would allot them a share in the doom's day catastrophes along with Philistia, Moab and Ammon, Ethiopia, and Assyria. However, because of His mercy a remnant of His people would survive.

During Noah's day God grieved over the worldwide corruption and violence. Since the minds of mankind were focused on evil continually, the only way to purge the earth was to destroy everything, "both man, and beast" and the polluted earth (Genesis 6:7, 13). Still, because of God's grace, His pronouncement of judgment retained hope. He preserved a righteous remnant, Noah and his family, who had found grace in the eyes of the Lord.

Thus we discover that remnant language is associated both with judgment and salvation. When God destroyed a wicked kingdom, He did not always annihilate everyone within that nation's borders. Instead, the wicked leaders and those under their influence were destroyed without remedy or remnant. And although the righteous remnant might suffer because of the destruction around them, God in His justice spared them.

B. On Judah and Jerusalem Because of Idolatry

Zephaniah began with a generalized pronouncement of judgment upon the earth, but in 1:4 narrowed the focus to Judah and Jerusalem. This prophecy focused specifically upon individual groups and explained the reason for judgment. Jerusalem, the seat of monotheistic worship of Jehovah, had become pagan in their worship. Their sin was manifold: those who practiced false religions; those who practiced a syncretistic form of worship by mixing Judaism and other religions; those who had forsaken the Lord and lived their lives apart from His commandments.

C. The Day of the Lord under the Figure of a Sacrifice

Some denounce God's right to judge, arguing that a loving God would never punish mankind in such a drastic way as Zephaniah and the other prophets proclaimed. Contrariwise, Zephaniah likened the punishment of sinners as a sacrifice to the God of justice (1:8). He specified those who would be punished: the royalty clothed in lavish foreign apparel, the violent and deceitful who violated their neighbor's rights, those with secure and careless attitudes, those uninterested in the things of God, merchants consumed with wealth, and those who view God as uncommitted to His creation. Judgment would strike Jerusalem without delay. This sure word of prophecy was fulfilled about twenty-five years later by the invasion of Babylonian forces.

D. The Terror of the Day of the Lord

Zephaniah pointed out certain characteristics of the Day of the Lord: it is approaching swiftly; it will be horrible (mighty men will cry bitterly); mankind's continual sin against God will be the cause; no one will escape apart from repentance and turning to God for mercy (1:14-18).

II. JUDAH CALLED TO REPENT

God, in His righteous judgment, had made up His mind. He had designated the day of punishment and would not cancel it. A person's only hope was to place himself in the protecting hand of God. The call to "gather yourselves together" (2:1) spoke of a solemn assembly for the sake of acknowledging sin and seeking God's mercy. Zephaniah gave three directives for those who believed his message and desired to be saved from the wrath of God (2:3). (1) Seek the Lord. God needs to be foremost in our lives. We must lay aside all other means of protection and with a singular heart serve only Him. (2) Seek righteousness. We should desire to know and obey God's Word. (3) Seek meekness. This is to recognize our inability to save ourselves; it is a call to submit to God and to totally trust the God of mercy to save us. Jesus' Sermon on the Mount stressed these three directives.

III. THE DOOM OF GENTILE NATIONS

We are cognizant of this spiritual principle: "For unto whomsoever much is given, of him shall be much required" (Luke 12:48). Judah and Jerusalem seemed either to forget or to presumptuously neglect this principle. But God, who loved them with an everlasting love, would commit them to righteous punishment in order to bring them back to Himself. They were His covenant elect; He would not let them go astray without trying to woo them back.

Transparency 1

Transparency 1 says, "All nations are subject to God's rule and are 'without excuse' (Romans 1:20)."

However, all humanity is the Lord's. All nations are subject to God's rule. Paul proclaimed of the Gentiles, "They are without excuse" (Romans 1:20). And though Judah was the covenant nation and would be punished for breaking their vows, other nations were not exempt from following the righteous rules of God. Zephaniah proclaimed a woe to Israel's border nations that they would fall into the same judgment as Judah. He pronounced upon each nation a specific woe that soon would come to pass.

A. The Philistines

Upon entering the Promised Land, Israel neglected to completely subdue the Philistines, the people of the coastal communities. Consequently, the Philistines had plagued the people of God for centuries. But now their day of reckoning had arrived, and they would be uprooted from their land. They had seen the mighty acts of Israel's true and living God but for centuries had refused to turn to Him. Therefore, they would be destroyed as a nation and shepherds would use their land for grazing their flocks. After Judah returned from Babylonian captivity, the Lord would give them the Philistines' land.

B. The Moabites and Ammonites

The Moabites and Ammonites were descendents of the sin of Lot (Abraham's nephew) and his two daughters (Genesis 19:30-38). These nations failed to follow God who had delivered them from the wrath poured out upon Sodom and Gomorrah, yet they spoke disdainfully of the Israelites who followed after the God of Abraham. These nations failed to repent of their sins against God; rather, they continued in ungodly practices and mocked those who walked according to the oracles of God's Word. Now God would mock them; they would be destroyed as Sodom and Gomorrah had been destroyed centuries before.

C. The Ethiopians

The Ethiopians had spoiled the peace of Judah in the reign of the godly King Asa. They came against Judah with a million-man fighting machine and three hundred chariots. God had not forgotten their deeds against His people. Now the sword of Nebuchadnezzar would destroy them.

D. The Assyrians and the City of Nineveh

Over a hundred years earlier, Nineveh, the principal city of the Assyrians, had been spared the wrath of God because they repented at the preaching of Jonah. However, they had quickly returned to their previous sins and God intended to visit them again, this time with judgment instead of mercy. They would not be spared.

IV. WOE PRONOUNCED ON JERUSALEM

Jerusalem was the center of the Jewish monotheistic faith. It contained the Temple of Solomon where all Judah gathered to worship. The privileged people of God knew the greatness of the name of the Lord and saw the smoke from the sacrifices to Jehovah ascending daily into the heavens. Still, the inhabitants of Jerusalem, those who should have been closest to God, lived in opposition to His Word. Even the closest of the close, the religious leaders who lived near the Temple and handled holy things, were corrupt. The law of Moses was all but forgotten, and the Holy Scriptures lay in an abandoned room of the Temple, collecting dust. The priests had neglected the Temple for so long it was in dire need of repair. Thus God spoke a direct woe to the people of the beloved city.

A. Jerusalem's Sins

The prophet decried specific sins: moral corruption, disobedience to His voice of correction (through His Word and true prophets), self-reliance, and distancing themselves from God.

1. *Disobedience.* The priests had ignored the sacred copy of the law of Moses for so long they had forgotten not only its exact location in the Temple, but more important, the precepts it contained. Jerusalem lived in willful disobedience to the Word of God. Further, this sacred city was the pulpit of the prophets, God's current mouthpiece, but the people ignored and persecuted the true prophets and instead listened with favor to false prophets who spoke appeasing words.

"Her prophets are light and treacherous persons: her priests have polluted the sanctuary, they have done violence to the law" (Zephaniah 3:4).

2. *Unresponsiveness.* The people had distanced themselves from God. They did not seek Him, preferring instead to consort with Jerusalem's moral filth and pollution.

"Woe to her that is filthy and polluted, to the oppressing city! She obeyed not the voice: she received not correction; she trusted not in the Lord; *she drew not near to her God" (Zephaniah 3:1-2).*

3. *Unbelief.* The basic prerequisite for serving God is to believe that He is (Hebrews 11:6). Jerusalem treated their God as if He did not exist and had no part in their lives. As long as they found pleasure, they did not care about the wickedness of their ways.

"I will search Jerusalem with candles, and punish the men that are settled on their lees: that say in their heart, The Lord *will not do good, neither will he do evil" (Zephaniah 1:12).*

4. *Impenitence.* They refused to trust in God; further, they rejected the voice of correction.

"I will also stretch out mind hand upon Judah, and upon all the inhabitants of Jerusalem; and I will cut off . . . them that are turned back from the Lord; *and those that have not*

sought the Lord, *nor inquired for him" (Zephaniah 1:4, 6).*

B. Greed of the Princes and the Judges

The prophet condemned four specific categories of leadership within Jerusalem: princes, judges, prophets, and priests (1:8; 3:3-4). These rulers were morally corrupt. The princes as roaring lions oppressed the people, probably extorting money from them and taking their land illegally. The judges as wolves ruled with cruelty and greed, taking all and gnawing the bone even to the morrow.

C. Levity and Treachery of the Prophets and Sacrilege of the Priests

The prophets spoke falsely, desiring popularity among the people. The priests not only abandoned their duties of the law of Moses and their responsibilities of the Temple, but they lived a life that did "violence to the law" (3:4), probably by living immoral lifestyles.

D. The Lord's Presence in Judgment

The prophet reminded Jerusalem that God was in their midst. He had not abandoned them altogether; instead, He would punish them for their iniquities in order to redeem them from their iniquities. As a further warning, Zephaniah reminded them of the Lord's punishment upon other nations who would not turn from their sinful ways and were now decimated and desolate.

Transparency 2

Transparency 2 states, "God's people who err and do not repent will meet the same end as the sinner."

He warned that Jerusalem had taken the same path and therefore would meet the same end. God's hope in His chastisement was that Jerusalem would, unlike the other nations, repent of their sins and return to God in righteousness.

V. MESSAGE OF HOPE TO THE FAITHFUL REMNANT

Transparency 3

Transparency 3 says, "God's wrath does not obliterate His mercy. He will destroy the wicked but redeem the remnant that trusts in Him."

As always, the wrath of God did not obliterate His mercy. He said, "Wait ye upon me" (3:8). (See Zephaniah 3:8-13.) We see in this passage a two-fold promise: God will destroy the wicked nations, but He will redeem those who trust in Him. The prophecy speaks of both Judah's return from Babylonian captivity after seventy years and of the reign of the Lord during the Millennium. In retrospect, we can see this prophecy probably spoke more regarding the end times than it did of Judah's return from Babylonian captivity, for Judah's return did not bring sweeping revival to the world as is indicated by these verses. Even Ethiopia (one of the most remote lands known in that day) shall bring an offering unto the Lord (Zephaniah 3:10).

A. Destruction of Wicked Gentiles

The destruction of ungodly nations will take place. Though we typically wonder at the collapse of nations and generally attribute their demise to some internal governmental flaw or poor decision-making, we should consider what the Scripture says regarding nations that resist God's Word. Though suggesting God will punish a nation for its sins probably would incur public ridicule, the Scripture clearly indicates He will do so.

B. Conversion of the Remaining Nations

The passage found in Zephaniah 3:8-13 calls attention to two major events. First, the sweeping Pentecostal revival of the twentieth century has brought together people of all nations that call upon the name of the Lord and serve Him with one accord. Second, during the final Day of the Lord as proclaimed in the Book of Revelation, all nations will be brought under the banner of the one true God of Heaven: "And the seventh angel sounded; and there were great voices in heaven, saying, The kingdoms of this world are become the kingdoms of our Lord, and of his Christ; and he shall reign for ever and ever" (Revelation 11:15).

C. Restoration of Dispersed Israel

God's call to Abraham came with a promise that He would bless Abraham and make him a mighty nation. God warned that Abraham's descendants would go into Egyptian bondage, but promised He would deliver them and give them the land of Palestine. God kept His promise but warned that His people must serve Him with their whole hearts, forsaking all other gods and walking in His holiness.

With the blessing came the pronouncement of a curse if they failed to abide by their vows to Him. Although God did send His covenant people into captivity, He never altogether abandoned them. We have seen two restorations of Israel. The first is their return to Palestine in 537 BC after seventy years of Babylonian captivity. The second is their rebirth as a nation in 1947 after their destruction by the Romans in AD 70.

D. Rejoicing over the Second Advent of Christ

Though Zephaniah's message predicted utter destruction, he ended his prophecy with a wonderful song of hope. (See Zephaniah 3:8-20.) He saw an exuberant people rejoicing in the God of their salvation. Further, though God seemed to have abandoned them because of their sins, He would someday dwell in their midst. God Himself would rejoice over them when they turned their hearts to Him.

Perhaps today we catch a glimpse of the fulfillment of prophecy as the Jewish people sing and dance together in worship to God near the site of their ancient Temple. Ironically, this place of worship is called the Wailing Wall as a constant reminder of the destruction of Jerusalem almost two thousand years ago, but still they rejoice in hope, for the God who promised will bring His promises to pass.

What many Jews fail to recognize is that the promised Messiah has already come. During Christ's triumphal entry into Jerusalem, they cried, "Blessed is he that cometh in the name of the Lord; Hosanna in the highest" (Matthew 21:9). But the priests and scribes hated Him for His claim to be Jehovah manifested in flesh. Further, when they handed Jesus over to be crucified by the Romans they, along with the majority of Jews, rejected the idea that this lowly, suffering servant could be their Messiah. Their concept of Messiah was a hero who would conquer all their foes and rule the world from Jerusalem.

When unbelieving Jews persecuted Jesus for healing the impotent man on the Sabbath at the pool of Bethesda, Jesus answered, "My Father worketh hitherto, and I work" (John 5:17). They understood Jesus was claiming to be God and hated Him for it. In reality, they should have recognized Him, for they had access to three powerful testimonies of His identity: the mighty works of Jesus performed through the power of God, the Father Himself bore witness of His Son, and the Scriptures testified of Him. Jesus said, "Had ye believed Moses, ye would have believed me: for he wrote of me" (John 5:46). (See John 5:36-37, 39.)

Someday they will recognize Him and rejoice.

"Sing, O daughter of Zion; shout, O Israel; be glad and rejoice with all the heart, O daughter of Jerusalem. The LORD hath taken away thy judgments, he hath cast out thine enemy: the king of Israel, even the LORD, is in the midst of thee: thou shalt not see evil any more" (Zephaniah 3:14-15).

Internalizing the Message

Although Zephaniah wrote specifically to those of his era, his prophecy also points to the distant future. The final Day of the Lord is imminent, and the message against sin is the same today as preached by Zephaniah 2,600 years ago. Whether it is ancient Judah and its neighbors or our current society, all sin will be punished without exception.

Thankfully, along with the pronouncement of punishment God always offers hope. "The wages of sin is death; but the gift of God is eternal life through Jesus Christ our Lord" (Romans 6:23). The substitutionary death of Jesus Christ on Calvary paid the debt for our sin. We "receive our wages" of death by partaking in a similitude of His death through repentance of sins. Through water baptism by immersion in the name of the Lord Jesus Christ, we are buried with Christ.

Finally, by receiving His Spirit with the evidence of speaking in other tongues, we experience new life through His resurrection. (See Acts 2:37-43.)

"We are buried with him by baptism into death: that like as Christ was raised up from the dead by the glory of the Father, even so we also should walk in newness of life" (Romans 6:4).

Having received such marvelous grace, the church should echo the proclamation of Zephaniah: Sing! Shout! Be glad! Rejoice with all the heart!

REFLECTIONS

- Discuss the dual application of Zephaniah's prophecy, both to the people of his day and to us in the present.
- God's Word and His righteousness justify His wrath and punishment. Discuss.
- Discuss reasons why God can rightfully judge and punish Gentile nations but He also can include them in Israel's glowing future.
- Job said, "Sorrow is turned into joy before him" (Job 41:22). Discuss reasons why the Jews today can sing, dance, and rejoice at the Wailing Wall.
- The wages of sin have not changed. We receive redemption only by partaking in a similitude of the death of Jesus Christ on the cross. Discuss.

Haggai— Replacing the Curse with a Blessing

10
week of
08.04.13

Lesson Text

Haggai 2:11-18, 20-23

11 Thus saith the LORD of hosts; Ask now the priests concerning the law, saying,

12 If one bear holy flesh in the skirt of his garment, and with his skirt do touch bread, or pottage, or wine, or oil, or any meat, shall it be holy? And the priests answered and said, No.

13 Then said Haggai, If one that is unclean by a dead body touch any of these, shall it be unclean? And the priests answered and said, It shall be unclean.

14 Then answered Haggai, and said, So is this people, and so is this nation before me, saith the LORD; and so is every work of their hands; and that which they offer there is unclean.

15 And now, I pray you, consider from this day and upward, from before a stone was laid upon a stone in the temple of the LORD:

16 Since those days were, when one came to an heap of twenty measures, there were but ten: when one came to the pressfat for to draw out fifty vessels out of the press, there were but twenty.

17 I smote you with blasting and with mildew and with hail in all the labours of your hands; yet ye turned not to me, saith the LORD.

18 Consider now from this day and upward, from the four and twentieth day of the ninth month, even from the day that the foundation of the LORD's temple was laid, consider it.

· · · · ·

20 And again the word of the LORD came unto Haggai in the four and twentieth day of the month, saying,

21 Speak to Zerubbabel, governor of Judah, saying, I will shake the heavens and the earth;

22 And I will overthrow the throne of kingdoms, and I will destroy the strength of the kingdoms of the heathen; and I will overthrow the chariots, and those that ride in them; and the horses and their riders shall come down, every one by the sword of his brother.

23 In that day, saith the LORD of hosts, will I take thee, O Zerubbabel, my servant, the son of Shealtiel, saith the LORD, and will make thee as a signet: for I have chosen thee, saith the LORD of hosts.

Focus Thought

Haggai's message gives hope that God can lift the curse of sin and replace it with the blessing of His Spirit.

Focus Verse

Haggai 2:19

Is the seed yet in the barn? yea, as yet the vine, and the fig tree, and the pomegranate, and the olive tree, hath not brought forth: from this day will I bless you.

Just Do It!

by Dorsey Burk

I know I can be impatient. I drove through the drive-through this morning to get breakfast. The girl at the window didn't even look up to acknowledge my presence but continued to read the sheets of paper on her table. She didn't seem to be concerned that I was in a hurry or that my fingers were tapping on the car door. Finally, she turned and with a big smile handed me my sack.

We face it all the time. Store clerks are too busy talking to each other to answer our questions. The bank teller closes her window to go on break when we are next in line. Kids shuffle and poke each other as they cross the street while we are waiting to turn.

Don't you just want to tell them to get busy?

I hope the Lord never feels that way about me. I want to be a faithful servant, always eager to do the Master's will. I don't want to get sidetracked with the cares of the world and lose sight of the real priorities of life. I want to always put Him first.

Ecclesiastes 9:10 states, "Whatsoever thy hand findeth to do, do it with thy might." A few years ago, Nike put a modern spin on Solomon's word. Nike said, "Just do it!"

I. FIRST PROPHECY—FOLLY OF NEGLECT
   A. Rebuke for Neglect in Rebuilding the Temple
   B. Results of Misplaced Priorities
   C. Encouraged by Haggai, the People Resumed Work on the Temple
II. SECOND PROPHECY—FUTURE GLORY
   A. The Prophet's Assurance of the Lord's Presence
   B. The Excelling Glory of the Future Temple
III. THIRD PROPHECY—BLESSING OF OBEDIENCE
   A. Discussion about Holiness and Defilement
   B. People's Scarcity before the Foundation of the Temple Was Laid
   C. Blessing to Accompany the Resumption of Work on the Temple
IV. FOURTH PROPHECY—MESSIANIC PROMISE
   A. The People Encouraged
   B. Zerubbabel a Type of the Lord Jesus Christ
   C. Curse Replaced with Blessing

Contemplating the Topic

Haggai's preaching augments the story of what happened when Zerubbabel and a remnant of almost fifty thousand Jews returned to Jerusalem after their exile in Babylon. They found broken, crumbling walls and buildings, and throughout the territory a sparse population of Jews, many of whom had not kept records of their tribal lineage, and Samaritans, the mixed race of Jews and other peoples the Assyrians had settled in the land almost two hundred years earlier.

The worst shock of all was to see the once majestic Temple lying in ruins. Although those of the remnant born during the Captivity had never seen the Temple, the elders who remembered its splendor mourned over the desecration. For seventy years they had longed to worship God and sacrifice to Him in the Temple, for this sacred dwelling place of God was an essential component of their covenant relationship with Him. It would have to be rebuilt without delay.

The younger ones had only a mental picture of Temple worship, concepts they had been taught by their parents and in the synagogues in Babylon. It was hard for them to imagine the priests performing ritual sacrifices in the Temple when all they saw was a massive pile of charred cedar beams and paneling, toppled pillars, and doors with hack marks where the gold overlay had been removed.

Zerubbabel had arrived in Jerusalem laden with the vessels Nebuchadnezzar had confiscated from the Temple, plus silver, gold, other precious things, goods, and animals. The Jews who had remained in Babylon contributed offerings, as well as non-Jews who had been encouraged by King Cyrus to do so. After the remnant arrived in Jerusalem, the elders also contributed lavish freewill offerings to facilitate the rebuilding of the Temple. (See Ezra 1-2.)

After the people had settled in Jerusalem and surrounding towns, they reconstructed the altar on its original base and began offering daily burnt offerings according to the Book of Moses. They kept the Feast of Tabernacles. Then they began the monumental task of clearing away the rubble so they could build the foundation of the Temple. They hired masons and carpenters, along with Sidonians and Tyrians to float cedar logs from Lebanon to Joppa to be transported to the Temple site, according to the grant issued by King Cyrus. Levites oversaw the building of the foundation to its completion two years after their arrival in Jerusalem.

To celebrate, priests blew trumpets and the Levites played instruments according to the order of David, king of Israel. Choirs sang praises to the Lord, and the people "shouted with a great shout." Anyone listening to the noise, which could be "heard afar off" would not have been able to distinguish between the wailing of the elders and the rejoicing of the young ones. The elders "who had seen the first house . . . wept with a loud voice" because this second Temple did not have the beauty and luster of Solomon's Temple, which had been one of the wonders of the ancient world. (See Ezra 3:8-13.)

The activity and commotion attracted the attention of the Samaritans, and they came to ask Zerubbabel if they could join in the construction, saying, "We seek your God, as ye do; and we do sacrifice unto him" (Ezra 4:2). According to *The Nelson Study Bible*, however, the fact the Samaritans did not use the proper name for God—Yahweh—suggested "their understanding of the Lord was still quite poor." Zerubbabel, Jeshua the priest, and the elders bluntly refused assistance from the Samaritans. "Ye have nothing to do with us to build an house unto our God" (Ezra 4:3).

This offense roused the Samaritans' ire, commencing a spiteful harassment of the Jews that "weakened the hands of the people of Judah, and troubled and terrified them in building, and hired counselors against them, to frustrate their purpose and plans all the days of Cyrus king of Persia, even until the reign of Darius [II] king of Persia" (Ezra 4:4-5, AMP). They wrote a letter to the Persian king warning him that the Jews, if allowed to rebuild and strengthen Jerusalem, would increase in power and rebel against the king, and he would no longer rule over the territo-

ries west of Jordan. They told the king to have the court records searched to prove their accusations. The king had a scribe search the records and found the history of Jewish insurrection and sedition. He ordered the Jews to give up their plans to rebuild the city walls.

Searching the Scriptures

The Persian king forced the Jews to abandon their plans to rebuild the walls of Jerusalem—but not to abandon work on the Temple. Still, after the dedication of the Temple foundation, it seemed lethargy enveloped the Jews like a dense fog swallows up a seafarer. Perhaps it was due to the negative reaction of the elder priests as they viewed the foundation of the second Temple.

Maybe the young ones, upon whose strength the construction relied, were discouraged by the tears and grimaces and wails of their elders. They may have thought, *If that's the elders' reaction to our efforts on the foundation, what will they say about the new Temple itself? Why continue to risk any more attacks from the Samaritans? If God wants us to rebuild the Temple, why are we having nothing but trouble?*

The people turned their attention to personal concerns. The energy that should have gone into beautifying the house of the Lord now went into decorating their homes. The reference to "ceiled houses" in Haggai 1:4 indicates the Jews had gone far beyond seeing to their basic needs by decorating their homes elegantly and living in luxury. They said, "The time is not come, the time that the LORD'S house should be built" (Haggai 1:2). They had lost their vision.

I. FIRST PROPHECY—FOLLY OF NEGLECT

The prophecies of Haggai are among the most precisely dated prophecies of the Old Testament, spanning a period of only four months in 520 BC. His messages, along with the prophecies of his contemporary, Zechariah, gave the people a powerful motivation to resume work on the Temple, and the work commenced only three weeks after the delivery of Haggai's first prophecy.

A. Rebuke for Neglect in Rebuilding the Temple

Regarding this time period in Israel's history, it is important to realize the continuance of the ancient covenant was, according to *Keil and Delitzsch Commentary on the Old Testament*, "bound up with the Temple." The Temple was a vital component of Israel's covenant relationship with God. The purpose of the Old Testament Tabernacle or Temple was clearly laid out in Exodus 25:8: "And let them make me a sanctuary; that I may dwell among them."

Transparency 1

Transparency 1 states, "To be indifferent toward the rebuilding of the Temple was to be indifferent about the presence of God dwelling among them."

To be indifferent toward the rebuilding of the Temple was to be indifferent about the presence of God dwelling among them. The Temple was more than a mere physical structure; it represented their relationship with God. Had they cared about their relationship with God, their top priority would have been to rebuild the Temple before anything else. Our priorities reveal the nature of our relationship with God.

Haggai told the people, "Consider your ways" (Haggai 1:5, 7). They needed to realize God had withdrawn His blessings because of their neglect of the Temple. The people had sown an abundance of seed but reaped precious little from their efforts; they ate and drank but never were satisfied; they bundled up but were never warm; they put money in their pockets, but it seemed to disappear. (See Haggai 1:5-7.) Apathy and neglect kept God's people from prospering. (See Haggai 1:9-11.)

B. Results of Misplaced Priorities

The people may have forgotten the principle of blessing and cursing found in Deuteronomy 28 where Moses said, "If thou shalt hearken diligently unto the voice of the Lord thy God, to observe and to do all his commandments . . . all these blessings shall come on thee, and overtake thee" (Deuteronomy 28:1-2). The blessings touched every area of their lives: their travels, business matters, harvests, livestock, their enemies, their spirituality, relationships, families, health, and social standing.

Then Moses warned of the curses God would send if the people did not observe and obey the commandments, and the list of curses was as comprehensive as the list of blessings. If only the people in Haggai's day would recognize the

"cause-effect relationship between their poverty and their neglect of the Temple" *(Evangelical Commentary on the Bible)*, they could once again enjoy God's blessings by resuming their work on the Temple.

C. Encouraged by Haggai, the People Resumed Work on the Temple

God, through Haggai's anointed prophecy, stirred the spirit of the people to action. As soon as the harvest was completed, they began organizing work teams and assembling tools. As they worked, Haggai delivered the Lord's message to the people: "I am with you" (Haggai 1:13). Moses received a similar message of comfort and encouragement as he began the task of delivering the Israelites from Egypt. (See Exodus 3:12.)

II. SECOND PROPHECY— FUTURE GLORY

Reference points in the past often can be used to measure events in both the present and future. This can be good or bad. If a person learns from his past, he can work toward a better present and future. However, if he believes the past was utopia, his present and future are doomed because he believes he never will be able to surpass the achievements of the past. Such an attitude defeats faith and causes one to discount the sovereignty of God, who is in control of the present and the future.

God's ways and timing are not our own.

When God's people looked back to compare the past glory of Solomon's Temple to its present deplorable condition, they became discouraged. Admittedly, Solomon's Temple was a feat never to be repeated, but God's plan was to lead His people to something far greater than the first Temple—the new birth!

A. The Prophet's Assurance of the Lord's Presence

The remnant thought their past outshone the present; however, God's work was not finished. Haggai encouraged the people to focus on the reality of God's abiding presence and help. Dwelling on past misfortunes would only diminish their faith in God's promises or in His ability to perform those promises in the present. God's ways and timing are not our own. (See Isaiah 55:8.)

Haggai delivered his second prophecy on the first day of the Feast of Tabernacles, which according to our calendar was October 17, 520 BC. He admonished Zerubbabel, Joshua the high priest, and all the people to "be strong . . . and work: for I am with you" (Haggai 2:4).

B. The Excelling Glory of the Future Temple

Haggai realized the people were comparing the present situation to the glorious days of their past, and through the inspiration of God's Spirit challenged them to look to a future more glorious than they could imagine.

Transparency	2

Transparency 2 quotes Haggai 2:9.

"For thus saith the LORD of hosts; Yet once, it is a little while, and I will shake the heavens, and the earth, and the sea, and the dry land; and I will shake all nations, and the desire of all nations shall come: and I will fill this house with glory, saith the LORD of hosts. . . . The glory of this latter house shall be greater than of the former, saith the LORD of hosts: and in this place will I give peace" *(Haggai 2:6-7, 9).*

III. THIRD PROPHECY—BLESSING OF OBEDIENCE

A. Discussion about Holiness and Defilement

Haggai knew that even after the Temple had been completed and dedicated, its physical existence would not guarantee that the people approached God in wholehearted worship. Therefore, Haggai addressed the priests at the beginning of his third prophecy, since they were responsible for interpreting God's law, teaching it to the people, and leading public worship.

Haggai asked the priests, "Can holiness be transmitted by contact?" The priests, knowing full well the guidelines found in Numbers 19:11-13, answered no. Haggai then asked,

"Can defilement be transmitted by contact?" The priests answered yes. These questions segued into the real issue: "So is this people, and so is this nation" (Haggai 2:14). By now they should have learned that their neglect of the Lord's Temple had contaminated every area of their lives.

B. People's Scarcity Before the Foundation of the Temple Was Laid

During their three months of working on the Temple, the people probably had seen many indications of God's presence but had not yet experienced the abundance of God's blessings. They were between harvests, and their half-empty wine vats and storehouses still suffered from the effects of the past fifteen years.

Haggai spoke a message from the Lord: "I smote you with blasting and with mildew and with hail in all the labours of your hands; yet ye turned not to me" (Haggai 2:17). Although they had worked tirelessly on the physical construction of the Temple, they had not yet given much thought to their need for spiritual revival.

C. Blessing to Accompany the Resumption of Work on the Temple

God instructed, "Consider now from this day and upward" (Haggai 2:18). God was pleased with their hard work but also wanted them to turn fully to Him and acknowledge Him as the source of all their blessings. From that day forward, their hope for the blessings of God would become a reality.

IV. FOURTH PROPHECY— MESSIANIC PROMISE

The messianic promise made to David is recognized in Zerubbabel being a descendant of David. However, the promise reached its climax in Jesus Christ, who descended from both David and Zerubbabel (Matthew 1:12; Luke 3:27).

A. The People Encouraged

Haggai's fourth prophecy followed on the heels of the third. Perhaps he perceived the people's speculation about how long the Temple on which they were laboring would remain standing. They had seen the ruins of the first Temple; how long would it be before another heathen conqueror tore down the second Temple?

Haggai encouraged the people not only to look at the present, but to gaze forward into the future blessings when God would destroy the Gentile kingdoms of the earth and establish His everlasting kingdom.

B. Zerubbabel a Type of the Lord Jesus Christ

Haggai used Zerubbabel to represent God's authority over all the earth in that Zerubbabel would become God's "signet" (2:23). The signet was an engraved piece of stone, porcelain, or clay attached to a ring or sometimes worn on a string around a person's neck or arm. The bearer could seal a document, a tomb, or a doorpost. Through Zerubbabel's authoritative spiritual guidance during these trying times, the people could be cleansed and blessed.

C. Curse Replaced with Blessing

When Christ rules in His kingdom, the curse of sin will be gone. Sin's scourge upon the human race will be replaced with the blessing of Christ's eternal healing. There will be no suffering or sorrow, no more sickness or disease, and no more hospitals or cemeteries. Heaven will be a place of joy and peace. This is the believer's hope. Today we labor to build up God's kingdom, but some sweet tomorrow we will enter into the place He has built for us.

Internalizing the Message

What can New Testament believers learn from Haggai's message? First, poor behavior or a poor performance will guarantee a poor result. Little or no prayer, minimum Bible reading, inconsistent church attendance, and selfish preoccupation will hinder one's spiritual life and result in very little satisfaction, joy, or strength. When our lives seem fruitless and empty, we should heed the words of Haggai and reflect upon our manner of living. Realigning our priorities and placing God's kingdom first will release God's blessings into our lives. (See Matthew 6:33.)

Second, we should realize that church work is not the work of the church. Certainly there is merit in obedience; but when the obedient motions become mechanical, they become meaningless. God hungers for an intimate relationship with His people. He yearns not only to be *with us* but *in us*. (See John 14:17.) It is important to keep the Lord's commandments, but it is also of vital importance to foster a vibrant relationship with Him. (See John 15:1-12.) He said, "Without me ye can do nothing" (John 15:5). A person who goes through the motions apart from any intimate connection with Him will accomplish nothing.

Realigning our priorities and placing God's kingdom first will release God's blessings into our lives.

Third, it is a mistake to think that time diminishes the potency of God's promises or His ability to perform them. "The Lord is not slack concerning his promise" (II Peter 3:9); that is, His promises are well-timed. For instance, God promised Abraham a son by his wife Sarah, but she did not give birth to the child until twenty-five years later. (See Genesis 18:9-11; 21:3.) Through a dream God promised Joseph he would one day rule over his brothers, but it did not come to pass until thirteen years later. (See Genesis 37:2-11; 41:46; 42:6-9.) God promised the coming of the Messiah, but Jesus was not born until the "fullness of time was come" (Galatians 4:4).

Fourth, just as God was with Old Testament Israel in the Tabernacle and Temple, His Spirit now dwells within the New Testament believer. We should celebrate the removal of the curse of sin through the death, burial, and resurrection of Jesus Christ. We should celebrate the privilege of experiencing the new birth through repentance, water baptism in Jesus' name for the remission of sins, and receiving the Holy Spirit with the evidence of speaking in other tongues. God is *with us* and *in us*, and He brings abundant blessings to our lives.

Fifth, just as God wanted Old Testament believers to be holy even as He is holy, He also wants New Testament believers to walk in His holiness. Living a holy life does not simply mean subscribing to a list of do's and don'ts. Obedience to biblical standards is important, but it more important that we live in relationship with Jesus Christ. If we are filled with the Spirit, we will reflect His glory to a lost world. Peter said the fulfillment of these "exceeding great and precious promises" was to partake in the divine nature of Christ (II Peter 1:4).

72

When Christ lives within our hearts, we will manifest the fruit of the Spirit. (See Galatians 5:22-25.) Obeying the Lord's precepts in tandem with His holiness brings blessing and spiritual productivity. (See II Peter 1:5-8.)

Sixth, if a person learns from his past, he can work toward a better present and future. However, if he believes the past was utopia, his present and future are doomed because he will be convinced he could never attain to the achievements of the past. Such an attitude defeats faith and causes one to doubt the sovereignty of God. God's Spirit challenges us to look to a future more glorious than we can imagine. Paul concluded, "For all the promises of God in him are yea, and in him Amen, unto the glory of God by us" (II Corinthians 1:20).

Transparency 3

Transparency 3 says, "For the believer, the glory of the future will be the second coming of Jesus Christ."

For the believer, the glory of the future will be the second coming of Jesus Christ. We can trust in the surety of that promise, "for yet a little while, and he that shall come will come, and will not tarry" (Hebrews 10:37). Believers who grow weary with earthly struggles can keep their eyes focused heavenward, "looking for that blessed hope, and the glorious appearing of the great God and our Saviour Jesus Christ" (Titus 2:13).

In Revelation 21:9-22:7, John described the New Jerusalem wherein he saw no Temple, "for the Lord God Almighty and the Lamb are the temple of it" (Revelation 21:22). He saw no war—only peace. John wrote of good news for mankind: "There shall be no more curse: but the throne of God and of the Lamb shall be in it" (Revelation 22:3). He saw no more curse—only blessings. Sometimes we think our best days are behind us, but God knows the best is yet to come!

REFLECTIONS

- Discuss the means by which God realigned the Jews' priorities when they neglected the rebuilding of the Temple. Discuss how this could apply to our Christian life.
- The Jews' indifference toward rebuilding the Temple reflected their indifference about the presence of God dwelling among them. Discuss how indifferent attitudes and focus on temporal things can reflect—and also affect—what is happening in our Christian life.
- As Haggai's message was vital to the Jews, so is the message of an anointed minister of God vital to the spiritual and physical well-being of God's people today. Discuss.
- If a person believes the past was utopia, it will undermine the success of his present and future. Discuss.
- To the Jews the Temple symbolized the presence of God in their midst. To Christians, the church is their spiritual hub where corporate worship, instruction, and edification take place. However, John saw no temple in the Holy City. Discuss.

11

Zechariah—Christ's First Coming

Lesson Text

Zechariah 11:8-17

8 Three shepherds also I cut off in one month; and my soul lothed them, and their soul also abhorred me.

9 Then said I, I will not feed you: that that dieth, let it die; and that that is to be cut off, let it be cut off; and let the rest eat every one the flesh of another.

10 And I took my staff, even Beauty, and cut it asunder, that I might break my covenant which I had made with all the people.

11 And it was broken in that day: and so the poor of the flock that waited upon me knew that it was the word of the LORD.

12 And I said unto them, If ye think good, give me my price; and if not, forbear. So they weighed for my price thirty pieces of silver.

13 And the LORD said unto me, Cast it unto the potter: a goodly price that I was prised at of them. And I took the thirty pieces of silver, and cast them to the potter in the house of the LORD.

14 Then I cut asunder mine other staff, even Bands, that I might break the brotherhood between Judah and Israel.

15 And the LORD said unto me, Take unto thee yet the instruments of a foolish shepherd.

16 For, lo, I will raise up a shepherd in the land, which shall not visit those that be cut off, neither shall seek the young one, nor heal that that is broken, nor feed that that standeth still: but he shall eat the flesh of the fat, and tear their claws in pieces.

17 Woe to the idol shepherd that leaveth the flock! the sword shall be upon his arm, and upon his right eye: his arm shall be clean dried up, and his right eye shall be utterly darkened.

Focus Thought

Zechariah predicted the first coming of Jesus Christ.

Focus Verse

Zechariah 9:9

Rejoice greatly, O daughter of Zion; shout, O daughter of Jerusalem: behold, thy King cometh unto thee: he is just, and having salvation; lowly, and riding upon an ass, and upon a colt the foal of an ass.

He's Coming; Be Prepared

by Dorsey Burk

Several years ago at one of the general conferences in Louisville, my wife was walking from the hotel to Freedom Hall. A young man ran up to her and asked, "Are you pre-trib, mid-trib, or post-trib?" (This refers to three beliefs about the possible timing of the rapture of the church: pre-tribulation, mid-tribulation, or post-tribulation.) She replied that it didn't really matter what she thought, but she certainly hoped God was pre-trib. The young man said, "Well, my pastor is post-trib" and ran on to the arena. We have laughed about this incident many times.

I know many could give long dissertations why they are pre-trib, mid-trib, or post-trib. I think I have heard most of the arguments. I agree with my wife; I hope God is pre-trib!

I can't give a timeline as to when Jesus will come. However, news headlines read like fulfilled prophecy, so I know it will be soon. I don't worry whether He'll come before, during, or after the Great Tribulation. I simply know Jesus is coming. I want to be prepared.

I. A CALL TO REPENTANCE
   A. Warning
   B. Cleansing
II. ZECHARIAH'S VISIONS
   A. Encouragement of the Workers
   B. Encouragement of Zerubbabel
III. THE GLORIOUS PROMISE
   OF ISRAEL'S FUTURE
   A. God's Covenant People Are Victorious
   B. The King Will Establish Universal Peace
IV. THE MESSIAH
   A. The Unexpected Messiah
   B. The King-Priest
   C. The Good Shepherd

Contemplating the Topic

> "The prophecy of Zechariah is profoundly precious to the Christian because of its unique Messianic emphasis and its panoramic unfolding of the events connected with the first and especially the second advent of Christ and the consequent millennial restoration of the nation Israel." —Merrill F. Unger

Zechariah was born in Babylon of a priestly family. He returned to Jerusalem with Zerubbabel and nearly fifty thousand other exiles, including the prophet Haggai. Nehemiah 12:16 indicates Zechariah had succeeded his grandfather Iddo as head of his particular priestly family, for his name was included in the list of the chief priests and Levites who returned to Jerusalem from Babylon. (Zechariah's father was "Berechiah, the son of Iddo the prophet" Zechariah 1:1.)

As mentioned in lesson 10, the younger generation rejoiced about the newly completed Temple foundation but the older generation mourned. To the elders, the second Temple would be small and plain compared to the grandeur of Solomon's Temple. This mixed reaction along with other factors dampened the workers' enthusiasm, and the work on the Temple ceased for about fifteen years.

At this juncture in Israel's history, Haggai was an elder and Zechariah was a young man (Zechariah 2:4). It is possible God paired an older prophet with a younger one to knit the people together into one cohesive group working for a common cause. Zechariah's first message followed on the heels of Haggai's second message, and they all had the same theme. However, the younger prophet's ministry outlasted the elder prophet's because Haggai died, leaving Zechariah the sole prophet in Israel.

Zerubbabel, leader of the remnant, was a stalwart and princely descendent of King David, but he never sat on David's throne. The last pre-exilic king of Judah had been Zedekiah, the cowardly and confused king who vacillated between rebellion and surrender when the Babylonians invaded. Zedekiah was caught while attempting to escape and dragged before the ruthless Nebuchadnezzar who slew Zedekiah's children before his eyes, blinded him, and sent him in chains to Babylon. Zedekiah died on the way.

The lack of a king gave great significance to the role of the post-exilic prophets, and since they were closely associated with the Temple, it became the rallying point for the community. "The liberality of Cyrus the Great and Darius I in religious matters gave the prophets a sphere in which their program of restoration could succeed" (C. Hassell Bullock, *An Introduction to the Old Testament Prophetic Books*).

While the focus of this lesson will be upon the prophecies of Zechariah that pertained to Israel, it is vital that we not miss the applications of his exhortations to the church today. As we reflect upon the first coming of Jesus, its fulfilled prophecies, and resulting glorious redemption, we can also look toward the second coming of Jesus with an attitude of revival.

In our examination of the Messianic prophecies of Zechariah, we will consider them in two lessons. Today we will examine the rebuilding of the Temple under Zerubbabel and the prophecies concerning Christ's first appearance as the Messiah. Although to some His rejection by the Jewish nation may appear to have been a setback or defeat, we look ahead to His ultimate victory at His second coming and Millennial kingdom, which we will study in depth next week.

As we reflect upon the first coming of Jesus, its fulfilled prophecies, and resulting glorious redemption, we can also look toward the second coming of Jesus with an attitude of revival.

Searching the Scriptures

The Jews had restored the altar on its original base and completed the foundation. Haggai's first and second messages had "jumpstarted" the rebuilding of the Temple; and at the time of Zechariah's first message, the people had been working on the Temple for about two months.

I. A CALL TO REPENTANCE

A. Warning

"Be ye not as your fathers, unto whom the former prophets have cried, saying, Thus saith the LORD of hosts; Turn ye now from your evil ways, and from your evil doings: but they did not hear, nor hearken unto me, saith the LORD" (Zechariah 1:4).

God had sent Israel and Judah into captivity because their wicked actions had obstructed His divine purpose. For instance, God said, "When for all the causes whereby backsliding Israel committed adultery I had put her away, and given her a bill of divorce; yet her treacherous sister Judah feared not, but went and played the harlot also" (Jeremiah 3:8). (See Jeremiah 3:6-11.) Throughout the history of Israel and Judah, the chief priests and the people had "mocked the messengers of God, and despised his words, and misused his prophets, until the wrath of the LORD arose against his people, till there was no remedy" (II Chronicles 36:16).

Thus the reference points of Zechariah's audience were their ancestors' folly and the ensuing exiles to Assyria and Babylon. The implication was that if Judah did not turn to God after the return from exile, God would turn away from them—and there would be no remedy. God would settle for nothing less than His people's heartfelt and sincere response to Him. (See Zechariah 1:3.)

B. Cleansing

Zechariah saw a vision of the high priest Joshua "clothed with filthy garments" (3:3). Joshua represented Israel in general, but the priesthood in particular. The people's confidence in the priesthood and its service needed to be restored, for the priests had "violated [God's] law and profaned [His] holy things" (Ezekiel 22:26). If the people had no faith in the priesthood, their efforts to rebuild the Temple and resume their sacrificial worship would be in vain.

Transparency 1

Transparency 1 quotes a portion of Exodus 19:6.

Israel's spiritual transformation could not come until after the people repented; thus

Joshua's cleansing signified the removal of iniquity from the land (Zechariah 3:9). If Joshua was cleansed and accepted, the nation would be also; but if he was rejected from priestly service, the people would be rejected as well.

At Mount Sinai God had said to Israel, "Ye shall be unto me a kingdom of priests, and an holy nation" (Exodus 19:6). Israel had forgotten this divine desire, but God would never forget His choice of Abraham's seed as His inheritance. The vision of Joshua applied both to Israel's present and future.

> *"The glory of this latter house shall be greater than of the former, saith the Lord of hosts" (Haggai 2:9).*

In Zechariah 1:6 the people "returned [repented]." While some commentators attribute this "returning" to Israel's forefathers, others such as *Zondervan Bible Commentary* understand it as the people's immediate repentance to Zechariah's message. The latter view seems most correct, as the former view removes a link from the chain of logic. It makes little sense that Zechariah would conclude the passage by telling of Israel's repentance after pointing out the nation's failure to repent as the reason for their punishment.

II. ZECHARIAH'S VISIONS

A. Encouragement of the Workers

The far-reaching implications of Zechariah's visions served to encourage the workers as they labored to rebuild the Temple. If their hopes of the coming Messiah and the future glory of Israel died in Babylon, Zechariah's visions resurrected them. It is impossible in the time allotted to examine in detail all eight visions, so we will highlight those that motivated the workers to look beyond the physical structure of the Temple to realize its purpose and meaning for the future, as well as their hope for the appearance of the Messiah.

The four horns and four craftsmen of the second vision (1:18-21) symbolized the downfall of the nations that had brutalized Israel and Judah and sent them into captivity. This, coupled with the third vision of a surveyor measuring the present city of Jerusalem (2:1-13), put new heart in the workers. The Jerusalem they saw around them was sparsely populated and surrounded by crumbling walls. But Zechariah's story of a surveyor carefully measuring the boundaries of the city conveyed the idea that someday Zion would become so populous and prosperous that the city limits would have to expand.

It meant a great deal to the workers, who were anxious to rebuild and fortify the walls of Jerusalem against attack, to know someday their city would not need walls, for the Lord's "wall of fire round about" and His glory in their midst would assure them peace and safety (2:5).

The four chariots and four compass points of the eighth vision (6:1-8) assured the workers that someday their Messiah would come and He would be declared Lord of the whole earth. (See Zechariah 4:14.) Since time began, the rebellious nations of the earth had not known that the only thing standing between them and judgment was God's forbearance. When the cup of God's wrath was full, He would dispatch His bronze war chariots to topple the kingdoms with military force, plagues, and natural disasters.

While the nations suffered punishment, however, Israel could bask in the light of God's favor. They had done nothing to merit the favor of God; their righteousness was as filthy rags. Time and again the people had sinned, been punished, called out to God in repentance, and promised to do better. Yet time and again they had returned to their sinful ways. Truly, God's unmerited favor came to Israel because of His "election of grace." (See Romans 11:5.)

B. Encouragement of Zerubbabel

God had assigned Zerubbabel the seemingly insurmountable task of shepherding fifty thousand people from Babylon to Jerusalem, a journey of four months. He then had to rally the people to rebuild the Temple while contending with fierce Samaritan opposition and following the dictates of the Persian king. He had to restore the courses of priests and Levites and see that they and their holy things were sanctified for the service of God (Ezra 6:18; Nehemiah 12:47).

Most pressing of all, Zerubbabel had heard Haggai's second prophecy, "The glory of this latter house shall be greater than of the former, saith the LORD of hosts" (Haggai 2:9). Zerubbabel knew he did not have the resources or costly materials to fulfill that prophecy. How could he accomplish it all?

Transparency 2

Transparency 2 quotes a portion of Zechariah 4:6.

The answer came to Zerubbabel in Zechariah's fifth vision of the golden candlestick flanked by and connected to two olive trees (4:1-14). The oil—or the anointing of God—supplied by the olive trees, would flow from the branches through the pipes and into the lampstand to fuel the lamps. Zerubbabel felt anointing flow into him as he listened to God's personal message to him: "Not by might, nor by power, but by my spirit, saith the LORD of hosts. . . . The hands of Zerubbabel have laid the foundation of this house; his hands shall also finish it" (4:6, 9). True to God's Word, the Temple was eventually completed in 516 BC.

III. THE GLORIOUS PROMISE OF ISRAEL'S FUTURE

A. God's Covenant People Are Victorious

The seventy-year sentence for the sins of the southern kingdom of Judah was over, but the northern kingdom of Israel was still serving time after having fallen two hundred years before Zechariah's day. In the first vision the angel of the Lord asked, "O LORD of hosts, how long wilt thou not have mercy on Jerusalem and on the cities of Judah, against which thou hast had indignation these threescore and ten years?" (1:12) God's answer brought comfort.

> *"Thus saith the LORD; I am returned to Jerusalem with mercies: my house shall be built in it, saith the LORD of hosts" (Zechariah 1:16).*

Beginning with Abraham, God has always chosen and will always choose His people on the basis of faith and covenant. (See Deuteronomy 4:37—God loved Israel's fathers and chose their seed after them; Psalm 89:3-4—God chose Israel to be a special people unto Himself; Isaiah 14:1—"The LORD will yet choose Israel, and set them in their own land.") The mercy of the Lord was tangibly evident in Judah's return from Babylon and in the rebuilt Temple. Moreover, the prosperity and population of the cities of Judah soon would grow exponentially. But had God forgotten the northern kingdom of Israel?

Zechariah's use of the names "Judah" and "Joseph" in 10:6 lets us know that someday the northern and southern kingdoms will be reunited. It is obvious Judah represented the southern kingdom, but less obvious that in this instance Joseph represented the northern kingdom. However, in Judges 1:22-23 "the house of Joseph" had a tribal connotation, just as Ephraim did in Judges 1:29. God will bring the reunited nations of Israel and Judah back to the land He had promised to Abraham. Even more remarkably, "they shall be as though [God] had not cast them off" (Zechariah 10:6). Israel will be fully restored and the cause of their alienation from God will be forgotten!

> *"Not by might, nor by power, but by my spirit, saith the LORD of hosts" (Zechariah 4:6).*

Before the Messiah comes, the Gentile nations will unite to deliver a final death blow against God's people. But God will deprive the enemy of their strength and overpower them. God will enable "the flock of his people" to win the victory over all their enemies (9:16) and enjoy His abundant provisions (9:11-10:1). The knowledge of these future victories served as a powerful motivation to the people as they continued working on the Temple.

B. The King Will Establish Universal Peace

The kingdom of God is the theme of Zechariah 9-14. While surrounding nations cower under the force of God's wrath (9:1-9), Jerusalem and Zion will rejoice in the prospect of their anointed king and the establishment of His kingdom. "Rejoice greatly, O daughter of Zion" (9:9).

Someday God will say, "It is my people: and they shall say, The LORD is my God" (Zechariah 13:9). The Jews will recognize Jesus Christ as Lord and renew their covenant with Him (Leviticus 26:12). Their spiritual renewal will usher in peace. God will once again shower His people with material blessings. (See Zechariah 8:12; cf. Haggai 1:10).

The domain of the Prince of Peace will extend outward from Jerusalem and He will judge among all the nations of the earth. They will convert their weapons of warfare to useful tools; "neither shall they learn war any more" (Isaiah 2:4). (See also Isaiah 9:6-7; 11:1-10.) No longer will war cut off people in the prime of life. Children will play unmolested and their elders will sit and visit peacefully and unafraid in the streets of Jerusalem.

The people saw these promises concerning their coming Messiah, but their focus only upon the long-term fulfillment of physical promises blinded them to the actual arrival of their King, whose first coming was primarily a spiritual event. Consequently, most of the Jewish people failed to embrace Him at that time.

IV. THE MESSIAH

A. The Unexpected Messiah

Transparency 3

Transparency 3 states, "Although Jesus did not match the Jews' expectations of their Messiah, He was their King-Priest and Good Shepherd."

Although Jesus Christ fulfilled all of the Old Testament messianic prophecies, the Jews did not recognize Him as their long-awaited Messiah because He lacked the royal robes, regal bearing, and prestigious retinue they expected. His plain tunic was woven in one piece from neck to knees, similar to the garments worn by priests (John 19:23-24). According to Josephus in *Antiquities of the Jews*, the priest's garment "was not composed of two pieces, nor was it sewn together upon the shoulders and the sides, but it was one long vestment so woven as to have an opening for the neck."

Jesus was "just, and having salvation; lowly, and riding upon . . . a colt the foal of an ass" (Zechariah 9:9; cf. John 12:13-15; Philippians 2:7-8). He was "meek and lowly" (Matthew 11:29). He had no home (Matthew 8:20). He drew His twelve disciples from lowly and/or despised occupations. Jesus told Pilate, "My kingdom is not of this world" (John 18:36). The looks and actions of Jesus did not match the Jews' expectations of their Messiah.

Moreover, the Jews who celebrated the triumphal entry thought their Messiah was about to break the yoke of Rome and set up His earthly kingdom in Jerusalem, from which He would rule the world. They exulted, "Hosanna: Blessed is the King of Israel that cometh in the name of the Lord"! (John 12:13). But a week later when Jesus was arrested and tried before Pilate they cried, "Away with him, away with him, crucify him" (John 19:15). As He hung on the cross, they "railed on him, wagging their heads, and saying, Ah, thou that destroyest the temple, and buildest it in three days, save thyself, and come down from the cross" (Mark 15:29-30). He did not measure up to their political expectations.

Even the disciples misunderstood the time sequence of the establishment of the Messiah's earthly kingdom. After His resurrection and after hearing His final teachings for forty days, they asked Jesus one last question before He ascended: "Lord, wilt thou at this time restore again the kingdom to Israel?" (Acts 1:6).

The first-century Jews did not recognize Him as Messiah and neither have the Jews as a nation recognized Him unto this day.

The thoughts of Maimonides, a rabbi and preeminent Jewish scholar of the Middle Ages, put forth the reason Israel did not recognize Jesus as their Messiah: "As for Yeshua of Nazareth, who claimed to be the anointed one and was killed by the court, Daniel had already prophesied about him, thus: 'And the children of your people's rebels shall raise themselves to set up prophecy and will stumble' (Ibid. 14). Can there be a bigger stumbling block than this?

"All the Prophets said that the Anointed One saves Israel and rescues them, gathers their strayed ones and strengthens their mitzvot whereas this one caused the loss of Israel by sword, and to scatter their remnant and humiliate them, and to change the Torah and to cause most of the world to erroneously worship a god besides the Lord."

Will the Jewish nation ever recognize Jesus Christ as Messiah and King?

B. The King-Priest

> "[Zechariah's] picture of the Messiah . . . is a prophecy of surpassing beauty and importance" (Charles L. Feinberg, *The Minor Prophets*).

God commanded Zechariah to take the gifts of silver and gold that were brought from Babylon, make a crown, set it on the head of Joshua, and pronounce, "Thus speaketh the LORD of hosts, saying, Behold the man whose name is The BRANCH" (Zechariah 6:12).

The BRANCH (Zechariah 3:8; 6:12; cf. Isaiah 4:2; Jeremiah 23:5) means "Shoot" or "Twig" and serves as one of the titles of the Messiah, the offshoot of the royal stock of David. Many prophets predicted a king-priest would reign in righteousness. Jesus Christ fulfilled the prophecies by taking both a royal and a priestly role. (See John 12:13-15; I Timothy 6:13-16; Hebrews 4:14.)

Repentance plays a vital role in spiritual restoration and revival.

As Zechariah crowned Joshua, God told him to say, "Behold the man" (Zechariah 6:12). These were the very words Pilate uttered about Jesus Christ when He presented Him to the people (John 19:5). The Targums, the Aramaic translation and paraphrase, renders Zechariah's phrase, "Behold the Man, Messiah is his name, who is to be revealed."

Zerubbabel's completion of the Temple signified a far greater future fulfillment:

> *"He [Christ] shall build the temple of the LORD; and he shall bear the glory, and shall sit and rule upon his throne; and he shall be a priest upon his throne: and the counsel of peace shall be between them [the offices of King and Priest] both"* *(Zechariah 6:13).*

This same Jesus who had been despised and rejected will be acknowledged as King of kings and Lord of lords. His kingly and priestly roles will function in complete harmony. He will rule in righteousness with no need of judgment or incarceration, for Jerusalem will truly be what God originally intended—a "holy city." (See Zechariah 14:20-21.)

C. The Good Shepherd

God told Zechariah to participate in a symbolic act by becoming the shepherd of Israel and "feed[ing] the flock of the slaughter" (Zechariah 11:4). In acting out this role, he typified the messianic Shepherd King who cared for the flock, even though it was destined for slaughter. The flock despised and rejected Him, so He withdrew His protection by breaking the staff of favor and revoking the covenant of restraint. This left the flock vulnerable to the cruel onslaughts of the nations (11:4-14).

The Good Shepherd asked for His pay, and with a deliberate insult the flock gave Him thirty pieces (shekels) of silver, the price of a gored slave (Exodus 21:32). Contemptuously, the Shepherd cast the money "to the potter in the house of the LORD" (Zechariah 11:13), symbolizing Judas's action when he flung the silver into the Temple. The priests used the "blood money" to purchase a potter's field for the burial of the poor (Matthew 27:3-10).

> *"They shall look upon me whom they have pierced. . . . In that day there shall be a fountain opened to the house of David and to the inhabitants of Jerusalem for sin and for uncleanness" (Zechariah 12:10; 13:1).*

The Good Shepherd will turn His rebellious flock over to a "foolish" shepherd (Zechariah 11:15) who will abuse and devour the flock, decimating it by two-thirds. The nations will band together to invade Israel, but at the crucial moment, the Messiah will "go forth, and fight against those nations, as when he fought in the day of battle" (14:3). He will establish His kingdom and reign as "king over all the earth: in that day shall there be one LORD, and his name one" (14:9).

> *"Every one that is left of all the nations which came against Jerusalem shall even go up from year to year to worship the King, the LORD of hosts, and to keep the feast of tabernacles" (Zechariah 14:16).*

The whole earth finally will realize the Good Shepherd was smitten for their salvation. (See Zechariah 13:7.)

"Look unto me, and be ye saved, all the ends of the earth: for I am God, and there is none else. I have sworn by myself, the word is gone out of my mouth in righteousness, and shall not return, That unto me every knee shall bow, every tongue shall swear" (Isaiah 45:22-23). (See Philippians 2:10.)

Internalizing the Message

Repentance plays a vital role in spiritual restoration and revival. If we do not repent, we cannot expect to enjoy God's promises for the present and the future. (See Psalm 34:18; Isaiah 57:15-19.)

"Let us not be weary in well doing: for in due season we shall reap, if we faint not" (Galatians 6:9).

What a tragedy that the Jewish nation refused to recognize Jesus Christ as their Messiah because of their faulty expectations! Likewise, many people in the world today have a faulty perception of Jesus Christ. Paul wrote, "If he that cometh preacheth another Jesus, whom we have not preached, or if ye receive another spirit, which ye have not received, or another gospel, which ye have not accepted, ye might well bear with him" (II Corinthians 11:4). Let us align our perception of Jesus and His gospel with the Scriptures.

Visions of future glory can encourage us in our kingdom work. Paul said, "Let us not be weary in well doing: for in due season we shall reap, if we faint not" (Galatians 6:9). (See also I Corinthians 15:58.)

Like Zerubbabel, we do not have the resources or the ability to accomplish God's kingdom work and win the victory over our adversaries. "But thanks be to God, which giveth us the victory through our Lord Jesus Christ" (I Corinthians 15:57)! (See also I Chronicles 29:11; I John 5:4.)

REFLECTIONS

- Discuss the spiritual meaning behind Zechariah's and Haggai's encouragement of the people to rebuild the physical Temple. How can we "rebuild" our temple today?
- Discuss the history behind the declaration in Zechariah 11:10. Can a "broken staff" (covenant) be mended?
- Many in the world today have misunderstood the person and gospel of Jesus Christ. Discuss possible ways in which we as Apostolic believers can have or can acquire faulty perceptions of Jesus Christ. How can we correct such perceptions?
- Visions of the church's future glory can inspire us in our kingdom work. Discuss.
- Discuss the impossibility of accomplishing anything for the Kingdom outside of the anointing and enablement of Jesus Christ.

12

week of
08.18.13

Zechariah—Christ's Second Coming and Reign

Lesson Text

Zechariah 14:1-5

1 Behold, the day of the LORD cometh, and thy spoil shall be divided in the midst of thee.

2 For I will gather all nations against Jerusalem to battle; and the city shall be taken, and the houses rifled, and the women ravished; and half of the city shall go forth into captivity, and the residue of the people shall not be cut off from the city.

3 Then shall the LORD go forth, and fight against those nations, as when he fought in the day of battle.

4 And his feet shall stand in that day upon the mount of Olives, which is before Jerusalem on the east, and the mount of Olives shall cleave in the midst thereof toward the east and toward the west, and there shall be a very great valley; and half of the mountain shall remove toward the north, and half of it toward the south.

5 And ye shall flee to the valley of the mountains; for the valley of the mountains shall reach unto Azal: yea, ye shall flee, like as ye fled from before the earthquake in the days of Uzziah king of Judah: and the LORD my God shall come, and all the saints with thee.

Isaiah 11:6-9

6 The wolf also shall dwell with the lamb, and the leopard shall lie down with the kid; and the calf and the young lion and the fatling together; and a little child shall lead them.

7 And the cow and the bear shall feed; their young ones shall lie down together: and the lion shall eat straw like the ox.

8 And the sucking child shall play on the hole of the asp, and the weaned child shall put his hand on the cockatrice' den.

9 They shall not hurt nor destroy in all my holy mountain: for the earth shall be full of the knowledge of the LORD, as the waters cover the sea.

Revelation 20:4

4 And I saw thrones, and they sat upon them, and judgment was given unto them: and I saw the souls of them that were beheaded for the witness of Jesus, and for the word of God, and which had not worshipped the beast, neither his image, neither had received his mark upon their foreheads, or in their hands; and they lived and reigned with Christ a thousand years.

Focus Thought

Jesus Christ is coming to earth again; and when He returns, He will set up His millennial kingdom.

Focus Verse

Zechariah 14:9

And the LORD shall be king over all the earth: in that day shall there be one LORD, and his name one.

Jesus Is Coming Again!

by Richard M. Davis

There are many different ideas about and interpretations of biblical prophecy, especially in these end times in which we live. While we may not ascribe to every conclusion or idea about the fulfillment of prophecy, it is interesting to observe all the writing and speaking about prophecy today. One thing becomes clear through it all: many people sense we are living in the last days of dramatic destiny; and whatever their conclusions, most agree Jesus Christ is coming again.

Prophecy writer Jack Kelley believes there are seven major prophetic signs of the Second Coming, and it is his conclusion all seven are in "some stage of fulfillment." In his January 2012 annual update, in an article he titled "Seven Major Prophetic Signs of the Second Coming," Kelley listed the seven signs as follows:

"1. Israel Will Be in the Land . . . Ezekiel 36:8-12, 37:21. . . .

"2. Jerusalem Will Be in Jewish Hands . . . Luke 21:24. . . .

"3. A Moslem Coalition Armed and Led by Russia Will Attack the Holy Land . . . Ezekiel 38:2-6. . . .

"4. The Ancient Roman Empire Will Re-Emerge as a Political Force . . . Revelation 17:9-10. . . .

"5. The World Will Embrace a Single Religion . . . Revelation 13:8. . . .

"6. The World Will Accept a Single Government . . . Revelation 13:3. . . .

"7. Babylon Will Re-Emerge as a Prominent City in World Affairs . . . Revelation 18:2-3"

(*http://gracethrufaith.com/*, accessed March 21, 2012).

Kelley offers a number of interesting viewpoints for those intrigued by biblical prophecy. We may not all agree on his or others' conclusions, but this we know: Jesus Christ is preparing us for His soon return.

I. THE SETTING UP OF THE KINGDOM
  A. The Return of Jesus
  B. The Reign of Christ
II. THE NATURE OF THE KINGDOM
  A. Peace and Plenty
  B. No Satanic Activity
  C. Feast of Tabernacles
III. THE END OF THE MILLENNIAL REIGN
  A. Satan Loosed
  B. Rebellion and War
  C. The White Throne Judgment

Contemplating the Topic

Zechariah prophesied of both the first and second comings of Jesus Christ, the Messiah. Last week we studied what the prophet had to say regarding Christ's first appearance as the Messiah; this week we will observe the prophet's words concerning Christ's second coming, an event believers today continue to watch for in these end times. Further, we will observe prophecies concerning the earthly kingdom Christ will set up upon His return.

There are some people who object to the doctrine of the Millennium since the Bible does not mention the word. However, neither are such terms as *rapture, substitution,* and *incarnation* found in the Scriptures; yet we know these truths are valid.

The term *millennium* comes from the Latin word meaning "thousand years." While the term *millennium* is not mentioned in the Bible, the term "thousand years" appears six times in Revelation 20 and demands our attention. The term *millennium* means "thousand years" just as the term *century* means "hundred years."

The Millennium is the one-thousand-year reign of Jesus Christ upon the earth. The Millennium will be the Sabbath (rest) for this troubled world. True rest comes only when Jesus Christ reigns supreme. In the Millennium Christ will institute a literal reign and a literal peace. The nations remaining upon the earth will enjoy rest.

There are those who spiritualize this truth, believing the coming kingdom is only a spiritual kingdom. However, when Adam fell in sin,

83

the curse came upon the entire universe. Since that time, the creation has been groaning and travailing in pain. For the curse to be lifted, the entire earth and all of nature must be set free from the judgment of bondage that came following the fall of mankind.

Paul made this clear in his Epistle to the Romans when he referred to the entire creation groaning and travailing in pain (Romans 8:22). If we were to claim that this kingdom was only a spiritual kingdom, then we also would be forced to conclude that the curse upon the earth is only a spiritual curse and has no literal application. This, of course, is folly. For almost six millennia this universe has suffered from the effects of the curse brought about by sin.

Jesus Christ is coming again!

The kingdom age will be very important in proving the authority of Christ and His supremacy. It also is essential that there be a literal reign of Christ upon the earth to vindicate His righteous judgments. In the conflict of the ages, it would appear Jesus could be defeated if it were not for the Millennium. This golden age and the triumphant coming of Christ to earth will prove for all time that Jesus Christ is the conquering King before whom every knee shall bow.

The blessed time of Christ's reign can only come about by Jesus Christ, the Prince of Peace, coming to earth Himself. Jesus Christ is coming again!

Searching the Scriptures

I. THE SETTING UP OF THE KINGDOM

A. The Return of Jesus

The Scriptures are plain in their teaching that the second advent of our Lord will be before the Millennium and that the return of the Lord is the blessed and living hope of the church.

It appears that the Bible describes two phases in the second coming of our Lord just

as there were two phases in the first advent (first in bodily form to all, then in His resurrected body to His chosen disciples). Apparently there will also be two phases in His second advent. However, they will be in reverse order to that of His first advent. In His return, He will first come *for* His saints; then later He will come *with* His saints. Both of these comings will be pre-millennial.

Transparency 1 quotes I Thessalonians 4:17.

The first phase is the appearance of Jesus in the air when He will take His church out of this world. This phase of His coming will be to receive His saints and to return into glory, taking them with Him. The same Greek word translated "to meet" is used in I Thessalonians 4:17 and Acts 28:15. It means "a going forth in order to return with." This thought is clearly detailed regarding the first phase of the Lord's return. We commonly call this the rapture of the church, and it is the blessed hope of the saints.

The second phase of Christ's return will be the appearance of Jesus to execute judgment when He returns to reign and set up His millennial kingdom. This coming will be in power and in great glory as He returns physically to the Mount of Olives. Several Scripture verses describe this full manifestation of the glory of Jesus Christ and the revelation of Christ as Lord and King to the entire world.

> *"When the Son of man shall come in his glory, and all the holy angels with him, then shall he sit upon the throne of his glory" (Matthew 25:31).*
>
> *"And to you who are troubled rest with us, when the Lord Jesus shall be revealed from heaven with his mighty angels, in flaming fire taking vengeance on them that know not God, and obey not the gospel of our Lord Jesus Christ" (II Thessalonians 1:7-8).*

The appearance of Jesus Christ in judgment is that which Isaiah referred to in his prophecy: "I have trodden the winepress alone; and of the people there was none with me: for I will tread them in mine anger, and trample them in my fury; and their blood shall be sprinkled upon my garments, and I will

84

stain all my raiment. For the day of vengeance is in mine heart, and the year of my redeemed is come" (Isaiah 63:3-4). When this is fulfilled, every knee shall bow and every tongue shall confess that Jesus Christ is Lord.

A vivid description of our Lord's return to earth is given in Revelation 19. He is clearly identified because His name is called "The Word of God" (19:6). It is none other than Jesus who will come to smite the nations and rule them with a rod of iron. He is described as treading "the winepress of the fierceness and wrath of Almighty God" (Revelation 19:15). On His vesture is written "KING OF KINGS, AND LORD OF LORDS" (Revelation 19:16). One of the characteristics of His return at this time should be clearly noted: "In righteousness, he doth judge and make war" (Revelation 19:11). His coming and the kingdom that He shall establish will all be in righteousness.

Accompanying Him will be the armies of Heaven. These are identified in Revelation 20:6 as those who have part in the first resurrection. They will be priests of God in the millennial reign and will reign with Christ one thousand years. They will come with Him seated upon white horses.

When Jesus ascended from the Mount of Olives, the promise was given that this same Jesus shall come in like manner as the disciples saw Him go into Heaven. (See Acts 1:11.) This prophecy will be literally fulfilled when the Lord returns to the Mount of Olives.

At this revelation of Jesus Christ, an angel will bind Satan and cast him into the bottomless pit for one thousand years. It is clearly stated that during this blessed time, Satan will not be able to deceive the nations. We may conclude that as the glorious kingdom age is established on this earth, Jesus Christ is primarily dealing with nations.

B. The Reign of Christ

Since Satan will be bound and no longer able to deceive the nations, the people will submit to a theocratic government, an authoritarian government ruled solely by Jesus Christ, who will rule with an iron rod.

The majority of people populating the earth during the Millennium will be unregenerate men and women. Although the kingdom will be a righteous one, men and women will be able to sin. At no time does God take away from humankind the prerogative of free choice. (See Zechariah 14:17-19.)

The form of government will be a theocracy; Jesus will be "king over all the earth"

(Zechariah 14:9). Although Jesus will rule with a rod of iron, yet obedience will come through respect and godly fear. During the height of power in the British Empire, England was able to maintain peace in many of their colonies by this means.

A former missionary to India told about observing times of riot when the British planes would appear. The aircraft would fly low over the crowds and in a few moments, peace would be restored. The crowds would be dispelled without the firing of a shot. This showed the respect and fear the people had for the British authority.

The seat of God's rule on the earth will be Jerusalem. (See Isaiah 2:2-4.) The saints will have authority to govern with Him. The word *reign* means "to govern." The saints will govern the world with Jesus for one thousand years, the seat of government being the New Jerusalem.

The knowledge of the Lord will fill the heart of every individual and holiness will be the main theme.

II. THE NATURE OF THE KINGDOM

A. Peace and Plenty

This earth has a bright and glorious future. Some day nations will no longer need swords, but will convert their swords into plowshares. Righteousness and peace will surely kiss each other and creation's curse and travail (pain) will end. Mercy and truth will meet together.

It will be an age of righteousness. "They shall not hurt nor destroy in all my holy mountain: for the earth shall be full of the knowledge of the LORD, as the waters cover the sea" (Isaiah 11:9). Zechariah also described the peace and righteousness of this future kingdom in Zechariah 14:20: "In that day shall there be upon the bells of the horses, HOLINESS UNTO THE LORD." The ungodly music of this present world will be replaced with sweet chimes of bells ringing out the message of holiness. The knowledge of the Lord will fill the heart of every individual and holiness will be the main theme.

Carnivorous animals such as the wolf, bear, and lion shall no longer eat meat but feed upon grass and herbs. Hatred and fear will be removed both from individuals' hearts and from animals. There will no longer be poisonous serpents. The children will be able to play safely everywhere. There will be no need for locks on the doors. Robbery, murder, and rape will be completely removed from the earth and all people will be able to dwell safely and without fear.

The Millennium is the one-thousand-year reign of Jesus Christ upon the earth.

B. No Satanic Activity

The Millennium is to be an age of righteousness. The only means to secure a righteous era is for Satan to be bound. As long as he is loose, mankind will be in trouble. However, God will send an angel to bind Satan and cast him into the bottomless pit.

Further, fallen angels are kept in everlasting chains under darkness awaiting judgment. (See Jude 6.) It is not necessary for us to speculate concerning the nature of these chains. It is sufficient to know the chain by which Satan will be bound is long enough and strong enough to hold him as long as the Lord determines.

The bottomless pit is not the lake of fire, which is the final place of eternal torment. Rather, it is a prison in which evil spirits are confined, awaiting final judgment. There Satan will be imprisoned during the Millennium. The object of his imprisonment is not to render his due punishment but to remove him from the earth and restrain him from doing evil.

Along with Satan, the demons who are now so active will be bound. Isaiah 24:21-22 states this clearly: "And it shall come to pass in that day, that the LORD shall punish the host of the high ones that are on high, and the kings of the earth upon the earth. And they shall be gathered together, as prisoners are gathered in the pit, and shall shut up in the prison, and after many days shall they be visited." This means Satan will be inactive and there will be no satanic forces on the loose during the Millennium.

Satan is a master of deceit and rebellion; but during the one thousand years of peace, he will be unable to use his evil forces to torment or destroy.

C. Feast of Tabernacles

The Feast of Tabernacles was the third of three great festivals of the Hebrews. It lasted for seven days followed by a day of holy convocation. This religious feast was set forth to be a thanksgiving for the harvest and a commemoration of the time when the Israelites dwelt in tents during their passage through the wilderness. Apparently this religious feast will be carried into the Millennium.

The importance of the feast is evident by the judgment that shall fall upon those who do not attend. Apparently the Lord will place great importance on the harvest feast and the spirit of thanksgiving that accompanies it. We may not comprehend the many spiritual applications of this future time, but it is sufficient to know God will compel all to keep the feast celebration. Punishment for disobedience will be the absence of rain upon the crops, and the heathen who refuse to keep the feast will be smitten with the plague.

III. THE END OF THE MILLENNIAL REIGN

A. Satan Loosed

Since peace and righteousness will finally dwell among all nations, many people might question the reason for loosing Satan from his prison. These same individuals might question the reason God placed the tree of the knowledge of good and evil in the Garden of Eden when He created mankind. Those who question God's purpose in this fail to see that God is glorified through humankind's free choice. In order for mankind to exercise this God-given right of choosing for himself, He must loose Satan and give individuals a final opportunity to choose between good and evil.

During the Millennium, children will be born and raised in a clean moral society. They will not know temptation to do evil, but at the same time they will need to experience the new birth and redemption if they are to be saved. Human nature in itself is incurably evil and not capable of self-improvement. Good works and morality are insufficient to save mankind. Humans must be changed by the power of regeneration by the Spirit of God.

During the Millennium, individuals will be willing subjects of the King of kings but will render only lip service. Their subjection to Him will be by restraint; therefore God must administer a final time of testing. To bring this about, He has to loose Satan for a season.

B. Rebellion and War

Deception and rebellion are two great instruments the devil uses in the destruction of humankind. In the beginning, he was able to deceive Eve, who lived in a state of innocence. Through deception he caused her to disobey God. At the close of the Millennium, the devil will find the world populated by millions who will be in a similar condition to that of Eve. He will quickly deceive the nations and cause people to rise up in rebellion against Jesus Christ.

This testing will prove that evil nature, whether confined in a prison or subject to righteous rule, does not change. Mankind within himself does not have the power to be moral and righteous. He will quickly fall into the snare set by Satan; then the final judgment will take place.

An illustration of what happens to the devil is found in the story of Napoleon Bonaparte. He was defeated near Leipzig in 1813 and was exiled to the island of Elba. In 1815, he escaped and soon the French armies were rallying to his leadership.

It took the Battle of Waterloo to finally defeat Napoleon. He was then exiled to St. Helena where he spent the rest of his life.

The one way Napoleon's story does not illustrate what will happen to the devil is that Satan will not escape. He will be set free after one thousand years and then, following a final defeat, will be cast into the lake of fire.

C. The White Throne Judgment

All sin must be judged. If sin is not remitted in this life, it will follow the individual into eternity. God's first judgment for sin was at the Cross; God's final judgment for sin will occur at the Great White Throne judgment.

Transparency 2 depicts Jesus on the throne and states, "God's final judgment for sin will occur at the Great White Throne judgment."

There will be a resurrection of all mankind who did not have part in the first resurrection. All who are raised in this resurrection will stand before God as the books are opened. These books are probably (1) the Word of God—the Bible; (2) God's book of remembrance where their works are described; (3) the Lamb's Book of Life. (See Revelation 21:27.) At this judgment, the eternal destiny of each person will be determined solely upon the basis of whether his name is in the Book of Life. The supreme question will be, "Is your name in the Book of Life?"

Internalizing the Message

Everything the Lord does and offers to the church is real. Salvation is real. The hope of the Christian is real. Jesus Christ reigning within our hearts at the present time is real. Likewise, Jesus reigning upon the earth during the Millennium will be real.

We shall not be some nebula of light floating in the Milky Way, but we are going to dwell in a real city, the New Jerusalem. The promise of our reigning with Him in His kingdom is real. The hope of the child of God is glorious.

Our God is a victorious King. His conquering power will be manifested when He returns to earth in glory and sets up His millennial kingdom. His righteous judgments will be vindicated and every tongue will confess that He is Lord.

Jesus Christ is coming again! It would behoove every individual to be ready to meet Him when He comes.

REFLECTIONS

- Discuss how the return of Jesus Christ is the supreme hope of believers for every generation.
- Discuss the purpose of the kingdom in God's plan for the ages.
- What are the two phases of the return of Jesus Christ? Discuss.
- Why will it be necessary for Satan to be bound during the Millennium?
- Why will it be necessary for the devil to be loosed for a short time following the Millennium?

13

Malachi—Honoring God

Lesson Text

Malachi 1:6-14

6 A son honoureth his father, and a servant his master: if then I be a father, where is mine honour? and if I be a master, where is my fear? saith the LORD of hosts unto you, O priests, that despise my name. And ye say, Wherein have we despised thy name?

7 Ye offer polluted bread upon mine altar; and ye say, Wherein have we polluted thee? In that ye say, The table of the LORD is contemptible.

8 And if ye offer the blind for sacrifice, is it not evil? and if ye offer the lame and sick, is it not evil? offer it now unto thy governor; will he be pleased with thee, or accept thy person? saith the LORD of hosts.

9 And now, I pray you, beseech God that he will be gracious unto us: this hath been by your means: will he regard your persons? saith the LORD of hosts.

10 Who is there even among you that would shut the doors for nought? neither do ye kindle fire on mine altar for nought. I have no pleasure in you, saith the LORD of hosts, neither will I accept an offering at your hand.

11 For from the rising of the sun even unto the going down of the same my name shall be great among the Gentiles; and in every place incense shall be offered unto my name, and a pure offering: for my name shall be great among the heathen, saith the LORD of hosts.

12 But ye have profaned it, in that ye say, The table of the LORD is polluted; and the fruit thereof, even his meat, is contemptible.

13 Ye said also, Behold, what a weariness is it! and ye have snuffed at it, saith the LORD of hosts; and ye brought that which was torn, and the lame, and the sick; thus ye brought an offering: should I accept this of your hand? saith the LORD.

14 But cursed be the deceiver, which hath in his flock a male, and voweth, and sacrificeth unto the Lord a corrupt thing: for I am a great King, saith the LORD of hosts, and my name is dreadful among the heathen.

Focus Thought

God desires that we honor Him and one another.

Focus Verse

Malachi 1:6

A son honoureth his father, and a servant his master: if then I be a father, where is mine honour? and if I be a master, where is my fear? saith the LORD of hosts unto you, O priests, that despise my name. And ye say, Wherein have we despised thy name?

To Honor God

by Richard M. Davis

According to Sterling Durgy, "Cain evidently thought that anything he brought to God should have been acceptable to God. He was concerned with pleasing himself by his offering, not God. When God pointed out that Cain was falling short, Cain's response was to become angry at both God and his brother. Cain's violence towards Abel reflected Cain's poor attitude toward God.

"Just as with Cain, what we give to God in worship is a part of our relationship with God. A good gift is one that blesses and pleases the receiver. Since God is the Creator and actually needs nothing from us, the reason to give has more to do with our relationship with God than with God's need for anything to be provided for His work (Psalm 50, Acts 17:24-28)" (*surfinthespirit.com*, "The True Worship of God: Giving to Honor God," Sterling Durgy, accessed March 21, 2012).

It is amazing how arrogant humans can become toward God, demonstrating their erroneous idea that they should have their own way, that they should get whatever they want, or that they should never suffer—in other words, that everything revolves around them. However, everything does not revolve around us. To honor God completely and with everything we possess is our chief duty and responsibility in life.

"Let us hear the conclusion of the whole matter: Fear God, and keep his commandments: for this is the whole duty of man" (Ecclesiastes 12:13). Living our lives for God is what gives Him the most honor.

I. HOW ARE WE TO HONOR GOD?
   A. With Our Worship
   B. With Our Substance
   C. With Our Praise
II. GOD HONORS THOSE WHO HONOR HIM
   A. The Midwives in Egypt
   B. Joseph
   C. Daniel
III. GOD WILL CONDEMN THOSE WHO DO NOT HONOR HIM
   A. Herod Smitten by God
   B. Nebuchadnezzar Judged by God
IV. HOW CAN MAN HONOR GOD?
   A. A Weighty Question
   B. The Instruction of Paul
   C. The Three Homes

Contemplating the Topic

Today's lesson concerns God's indictment of Israel for failing to honor Him. The nation of Israel might honor its parents or masters but the people saw no reason to honor God. They acted out their contempt by offering to Him polluted bread and blind, lame, and sick animal sacrifices. Israel profaned the name of the Lord by saying, "The table of the LORD is polluted; and the fruit thereof, even his meat, is contemptible" (Malachi 1:12). They added insult to injury by "snuffing at," or dishonoring, their offering to the Lord by saying, "What a weariness is it!" (Malachi 1:13).

In this lesson we will study how we are to honor God with our worship, substance, praise, and our very lives. God honors those who honor Him and, conversely, He condemns those who do not honor Him. It is important that we learn how to honor God, for doing so is the quintessence of our salvation.

During World War II, a recruit in training refused to salute an officer who was of a race he did not respect. The officer took off the coat of his uniform, hung it on a post, and ordered the recruit to salute it one hundred times. The officer told him he was not saluting a man but the country that the uniform represented. We must remember that proper honor of God requires us to respect the people who represent His kingdom. When Israel wanted a king against God's will, Samuel told them they were not rejecting him, they were rejecting God as their king. (See I Samuel 8:7.) Let us so live that honoring God will be our daily desire.

I. HOW ARE WE TO HONOR GOD?

Transparency 1

Transparency 1 lists three ways that we honor God.

A. With Our Worship

Honor is defined as "great respect." Our worship of God is an outgrowth of our respect of Him. No one can worship God who does not first honor Him. If there is a deficiency in our honor, there will be a deficiency in our worship, for honor is worship in its embryonic stage. Honor becomes worship only when manifested in action. Thus honor alone could be called "passive worship," but God wants active worship. Although thoughts are not considered actions, if we pray to Him in our thoughts it is worship, for we are expressing our thoughts to Him. On the other hand, if worship never goes farther than a person's thoughts, that worship is lacking. We should endeavor to worship God in both thought and action.

Observing the fervent actions of the worshipers of false gods should give us pause. Many of these adherents to false religions go to great lengths to worship a god that does not exist. Many embark on pilgrimages or inflict pain upon their bodies in hopes of placating their gods. They enrich the temples of their gods by offering their substance while they themselves live in poverty. How much more should we express our enthusiasm and dedication to Jesus Christ, the only true and living God manifested in flesh!

B. With Our Substance

> "Honour the LORD with thy substance, and with the firstfruits of all thine increase" (Proverbs 3:9).

If we love God with all our heart, we will worship and honor Him with our substance. To love God completely is to have no thought of withholding from Him that which He has generously supplied. The word *substance* in Proverbs 3:9 means "wealth." We can honor God with our wealth by obeying Malachi's mandate to give tithes and offerings. (See Malachi 3:8-10.) If we have a healthy respect for God, we will give promptly, willingly, and cheerfully.

> "Every man according as he purposeth in his heart, so let him give; not grudgingly, or of necessity: for God loveth a cheerful giver" (II Corinthians 9:7). (See also Psalm 96:8-9.)

From the story of the rich young ruler we learn that reluctance to obey the Lord in financial matters reveals a spiritual problem. The excited young ruler ran to Jesus, asking Him what he should do to inherit eternal life. He told Jesus he had obeyed the commandments since he was a child. Jesus looked at him with love and said, "Go thy way, sell whatsoever thou hast, and give to the poor, and thou shalt have treasure in heaven: and come, take up the cross, and follow me" (Mark 10:21). The young man's smile turned to a frown and he walked away sorrowfully, for he counted his wealth a greater treasure than following Jesus.

If we love God with all our heart, we will worship and honor Him with our substance.

Our ability to give—or not give—of our substance is a litmus test of our spirituality. Many will give of their time and talent but balk when asked to give of their substance. Knowing this, Jesus taught more about money than He did about Heaven or Hell. Eleven of the thirty-nine parables of the New Testament address the issue of money.

C. With Our Praise

> "I will sing unto the LORD as long as I live: I will sing praise to my God while I have my being. My meditation of him shall be sweet: I will be glad in the LORD" (Psalm 104:33-34).

We have established that worship can be silent as we meditate on Him; but when our meditation manifests itself, the result is praise. We lift our hands and sing (Psalms 63:4; 104:33; 134:2), clap our hands and shout unto God with a voice of triumph (Psalm 47:1), dance before Him (Psalm 149:3), and kneel before Him in submission (Psalm 95:6). The Book of Psalms contains more than 150 references to praise.

> This writer pastored a man who was born without arms. During the altar service one night the pastor saw a touching sight. This young man who had no hands or arms to raise to Jesus was lying on his back with his feet raised in worship to the One who had saved him. This was an extraordinary example of honoring Jesus Christ with praise.

II. GOD HONORS THOSE WHO HONOR HIM

God not only is the great emancipator, He also is a great reciprocator. We think we know how to give back in return, but God's ability surpasses all of us in this area. For example, the Bible commands and promises, "Give, and it shall be given unto you" (Luke 6:38). The Word admonishes, "Draw nigh to God, and he will draw nigh to you" (James 4:8), and "Whosoever therefore shall confess me before men, him will I confess also before my Father which is in heaven" (Matthew 10:32). Let us not forget the Bible warns, "If we deny him, he also will deny us" (II Timothy 2:12).

Transparency 2

Transparency 2 quotes a portion of Psalm 1:1-3.

A. The Midwives in Egypt

After four centuries in Egyptian bondage, the number of Israelites had multiplied to the extent the new Pharaoh who did not know Joseph feared that the swelling Israeli population would pose a problem in time of war. In a military conflict the slaves could join the enemy and fight against Egypt. The new Pharaoh devised several diabolical methods to control the Hebrew population, one of which was to instruct the Hebrew midwives to kill the boy babies at birth. The Hebrew midwives feared God more than Pharaoh and chose to keep the male babies alive. When the king called them into question, they asserted, "The Hebrew women are not as the Egyptian women; for they are lively, and are delivered ere the midwives come in unto them" (Exodus 1:7).

God blessed the courageous and faithful midwives by providing households for them and establishing their families, a blessing normally reserved for men. (See Exodus 1:20-21.)

> *"Therefore God dealt well with the midwives: and the people multiplied, and waxed very mighty. And it came to pass, because the midwives feared God, that he made them houses" (Exodus 1:20-21).*

The midwives spared the life of Moses, and about eighty years later he delivered the midwives' children from the bondage of Egypt. Honoring God always reaps benefits, but these benefits are not always immediately evident.

B. Joseph

The story of Joseph is one of the most dramatic stories of the Bible. To his jealous brothers, Joseph's dreams made him look egotistical and arrogant, and they hated him. They tried to turn Joseph's dream into a nightmare by throwing him into a pit and selling him into slavery. He served as a slave in Potiphar's house, and then served an undeserved prison term in Pharaoh's dungeon. Even his rapid elevation to the palace did not fulfill the dream God had given him as a boy.

But regardless of the sorrow of being separated from his family and the hardships in Egypt, he honored God. One day when Joseph was almost forty years old, God fulfilled his dream by bringing Joseph's brothers and father to Egypt to bow down before him. He forgave his brothers' treachery and sustained them and their families during a great famine. (See Genesis 37-47.)

Paul wrote, "Let us not be weary in well doing: for in due season we shall reap, if we faint not" (Galatians 6:9). We can be encouraged that when we honor God by doing His will, regardless of the immediate outcome or circumstances, He will eventually fulfill His promises. "Let us hold fast the profession of our faith without wavering; (for he is faithful that promised;)" (Hebrews 10:23).

C. Daniel

Daniel, a young Jewish man taken into Babylonian captivity, honored God by refusing to defile himself with the king's meat and by making it a lifetime habit to pray three times each day. King Darius noted Daniel's integrity and wisdom and placed him in the upper echelon of the Medo-Persian government. (See Daniel 1:8; 6:10.) The king "preferred [Daniel] above the presidents and princes, because an excellent spirit was in him; and the king thought to set him over the whole realm" (Daniel 6:3). This obviously created jealousy among the presidents and princes, for they sought an occasion against Daniel. Finding none, they decided to engineer a way to destroy Daniel through his obedience to the law of God.

The presidents and princes went to the king with a request that he establish a royal statute: if anyone in the kingdom within the next thirty days asked a petition of any god or man save the king, he should be cast into the den of lions. However, Daniel's knowledge of the decree did not curtail his habit of opening his window and praying toward Jerusalem three times a day.

> *There is always a*
> *reward for faithfulness.*

The conspirators ran to inform the king of Daniel's violation of the decree, and Darius had no choice but to cast him into the den of lions because the laws of the Medes and Persians could not be changed. The king worried and paced all night, and when the dawn came, he hurried to the lions' den. "O Daniel, servant of the living God, is thy God . . . able to deliver thee from the lions?" (Daniel 6:20). Daniel assured the king he was fine. God blessed Daniel, the man who honored Him, by sparing him and extending his honored position throughout the reigns of Nebuchadnezzar, Belshazzar, Cyrus the Persian, and Darius the Mede.

Let us learn a lesson from these faithful people. There is always a reward for faithfulness. If we will stand by God, He will stand by us. He reciprocates the honor we give Him.

III. GOD WILL CONDEMN THOSE WHO DO NOT HONOR HIM

A. Herod Smitten by God

King Herod Agrippa I probably delivered many pompous speeches, but one fateful day he delivered his last. Sitting on his throne and arrayed in royal apparel, his speech so impressed the multitude that they shouted, "It is the voice of a god, and not of a man" (Acts 12:22). Because Herod accepted and enjoyed the accolades to deity, God smote him with worms and he died a shocking death "because he gave not God the glory" (Acts 12:23).

We never should take glory for our own successes, even though we feel we have earned recognition for doing excellent work. God deserves the glory for anything we accomplish in life, as He is the One who enabled us to achieve the success. Paul said, "Whatsoever ye do, do all to the glory of God" (I Corinthians 10:31). We should strive to be successful but prudent enough to give God all the glory when success comes.

B. Nebuchadnezzar Judged by God

Intoxicated with the elixir of power, Nebuchadnezzar boasted of his own greatness. "Is not this great Babylon, that I have built for the house of the kingdom by the might of my power, and for the honour of my majesty?" (Daniel 4:30). Although Nebuchadnezzar had admitted the sovereignty of God at the deliverance of the three Hebrew men from the fiery furnace, he still was proud and conceited.

God snatched every semblance of arrogance and sanity from the king's mind and banished him to live with the beasts of the field. He ate grass like an ox; his hair sprouted out like eagles' feathers and his nails grew into talons. This condition continued until he finally acknowledged God as the king of the universe. (See Daniel 4.)

Paul said, "Let nothing be done through strife or vainglory" (Philippians 2:3). *Vainglory* is translated from a Greek word meaning "empty pride" or "a desire for praise." Both Herod and Nebuchadnezzar gloated about their successes in order to reap the glory and praise of men. God condemned these two men because they heaped honor and glory to themselves instead of glorifying God for their works.

Failure to honor God reaps judgment. If we do not receive the judgment of God in this life, there awaits us a certain judgment. "And it is appointed unto men once to die, but after this the judgment" (Hebrews 9:27).

IV. HOW CAN MAN HONOR GOD?

A. A Weighty Question

If a dignitary were to visit our city and we were responsible for meeting and escorting him to comfortable lodgings, we would need to learn the necessary protocol.

Many years ago Missionary Billy Cole received an invitation to the palace to meet the king of Thailand. He was required to study a manual to learn the expected protocol and attire for the august occasion. Brother Cole learned he had to keep his eyes focused on the king at all times lest the king get the impression Brother Cole thought there was something in the room more important than the king.

We are entertaining a much more august and powerful personage than any earthly king: the Creator of the universe. For this reason we need to know how to honor God. Such knowledge does not come automatically. We must teach our children proper respect for God and His house.

B. The Instruction of Paul

"Unto him be glory in the church by Christ Jesus throughout all ages, world without end" (Ephesians 3:21).

Ephesians 3:21 makes it clear God is glorified through His church. When we were born of the Spirit, we became a glorifier of Him in this world. Being a part of the body of Christ enables us to honor Him in the greatest venue possible.

Transparency 3

Transparency 3 states, "Corporate worship of the church magnifies each individual's praise."

Worshiping and praising God with His corporate church acts similarly to the soundboard of a piano, which magnifies acoustic energy into the air. Without the "soundboard" of the church, one person's praise would be no louder than the muffled sound of a piano's hammer striking a string, and it would be drowned out by the clamor of the world's voices.

Paul admonished the church to "be filled with all the fulness of God" (Ephesians 3:19). Everyone can and should honor God individually, but one person's capacity for the fullness of God is limited. However, the global church body with Jesus Christ as the head can praise God with voices raised in a great crescendo.

"For all things are for your sakes, that the abundant grace might through the thanksgiving of many redound to the glory of God" (II Corinthians 4:15).

The Amplified New Testament renders II Corinthians 4:15, "For all [these] things are [taking place] for your sake, so that the more the grace . . . extends to more and more people and multiplies through the many, the more the thanksgiving may increase [and redound] to the glory of God."

C. The Three Homes

The rich and the famous of the world often boast of owning several homes in strategic parts of the world for their enjoyment as they travel. But not everyone can afford more than one home. Many of us are happy to have just one home. However, God knows every human actually needs three homes: a domestic home, a church home, and an eternal home.

First, God wants everyone to have a domestic home, for it is the bulwark of a godly society. In the home, we establish the basic moral and spiritual fiber that goes into the making of a Christian. Parents should teach their children truths that establish principles that make them not only better Christians, but better citizens.

Second, God wants everyone to have a church home. "Not forsaking the assembling of ourselves together, as the manner of some is; but exhorting one another: and so much the more, as ye see the day approaching" (Hebrews 10:25). We are to be faithful to our church home, for our church establishes within us truths that we might be able to please the Lord and be saved.

A pastor not only instructs but also protects the souls of church members and warns them of lurking dangers.

Some individuals never settle into a church home; therefore, they never learn how vital a pastor is—not only to them, but to their family. "Obey them that have the rule over you, and submit yourselves: for they watch for your souls, as they that must give account, that they may do it with joy, and not with grief: for that is unprofitable for you" (Hebrews 13:17). A pastor not only instructs but also protects the souls of church members and warns them of lurking dangers.

The third home is our eternal home. We are to live in such a way that we will be guaranteed an eternal home in Heaven. Our homes here on earth are temporal, but the reality that we have an eternal home comforts us.

"For we know that if our earthly house of this tabernacle were dissolved, we have a building of God, an house not made with hands, eternal in the heavens" (II Corinthians 5:1).

A pastor and his wife were called to the bedside of an elderly Indian woman who was dying. As they prayed with her, they heard her attempting to say something and leaned over. They barely heard her say, "I've got a home."

"Let not your heart be troubled: ye believe in God, believe also in me. In my Father's house are many mansions: if it were not so, I would have told you. I go to prepare a place for you. And if I go and prepare a place for you, I will come again, and receive you unto myself; that where I am, there ye may be also" (John 14:1-3).

Internalizing the Message

Human instinct does not teach us the proper ways to honor and please God. For instance, people all around the world conduct pilgrimages, reenact the sufferings of Christ on the cross, or mutilate their bodies in an effort to earn God's favor. Members of false religions burn incense and offer gifts to idols, grovel on mats on the floor, chant, or recite memorized prayers. Some extremists even kill people in their efforts to please "God."

We should thank God for revealing to us the truths in His Word through a pastor who teaches us how to honor God in our daily lives. Today's lesson has offered several key components of honoring God.

1. Worshiping sincerely and fervently. "I will praise the LORD with my whole heart, in the assembly of the upright, and in the congregation" (Psalm 111:1).

2. Giving of our substance—tithes and offerings. Failure in this area indicates a spiritual problem. "Every man according as he purposeth in his heart, so let him give; not grudgingly, or of necessity: for God loveth a cheerful giver" (II Corinthians 9:7).

3. Being faithful to a church home. "Those that be planted in the house of the LORD shall flourish in the courts of our God" (Psalm 92:13).

4. Living a consecrated life. "The steps of a good man are ordered by the LORD: and he delighteth in his way" (Psalm 37:23).

REFLECTIONS

- Discuss the ways our relationship with God is reciprocal, especially in the matter of honoring God.
- After we have honored God to the best of our ability, the honor we receive from Him is not always immediately apparent. Discuss, using the life of Joseph as an example.
- Is tithing really necessary? Discuss God's financial plan and why falling short in this area indicates a spiritual problem.
- Discuss how worshiping and praising along with a corporate church body increases our glorification of God.
- Discuss Paul's teaching in I Corinthians 10:31: "Whatsoever ye do, do all to the glory of God."